From Field to Town

Vincent Nicholas Rossi

FROM FIELD TO TOWN

Chronicles of North County History

STORYSEEKERS
San Diego, California

ISBN 978-0-9822671-0-3

Library of Congress Control Number: 2008911405

Published by StorySeekers
PO Box 27343
San Diego, CA 92198-1343
storyseekers@sbcglobal.net
www.story-seekers.com

Front cover: The Community Church of Poway, 1916,
photo courtesy of the Poway Historical and Memorial Society

To Peggy
in love and gratitude

Contents

Preface ix

Lime Street School 3

The McFeron story 5

Dining, dancing and fishing at Lake Hodges 7

The stars of Valley Center 10

The oldest Protestant church in Escondido 12

The little old schoolhouse 15

Camp Vista 17

The Escondido Hotel: A luxury destination 20

Olive days 22

An immigrant's dream 24

Patriarch of Palomar Mountain ranchers 27

Silk and sunshine 29

Melancton Barnett: business man and civic leader . . . 31

A lot of history in a little church 33

You knew you were home when you saw the tepee . . 36

Castle in the canyon 38

The town of Barham 40

The Cupeño expulsion 42

Elmer Field: a skilled mechanic 44

Sickler Brothers Mill 47

Water made the difference 49

Fallbrook's lost landmark 51

The telephone comes to town 54

The Old Richland School 56

"A representative cowboy" 58

Harry Tassell: a do-er, not a talker 60

The tragedy of Rancho Pauma 62

General store and more 64

When Rancho Bernardo was still a ranch 67

The Oden family: triumphs and tragedies 69

"The best of my life" 71

Homer Williams: He helped bring water to Poway . . 73

Built from the soil 76

Home run king from Escondido 78

North County Historical Societies
Museums and Libraries 81

Further resources 83

Index 97

Preface

This book is a compilation of articles that first appeared in the *San Diego Union-Tribune*'s "The Way We Were" column.

Reflecting on the history I've uncovered in researching and writing these articles, I'm struck by the parallels we can find between the lives of those in the past and our own. It's become fashionable in the era in which I am writing to speak of "career transitions" and people "reinventing themselves" in response to changes in the workplace. My move into freelance journalism after decades in corporate finance departments represented such a "career transition."

In reading these articles, it becomes obvious that many of those who settled in San Diego County in centuries past were "reinventing themselves" long before that phrase was invented. Many came from different parts of the United States or other parts of the world. Some came with almost nothing in the way of money or possessions and were able to transform themselves into successful farmers or small businessman. Some who were already comfortable made new fortunes as entrepreneurs and shared their success with their communities.

The articles tell about communities which began as isolated rural settlements whose residents struggled to survive as farmers and ranchers amid unforgiving cycles of drought and rainfall. Those who hung on built schools, hotels, and other institutions as some of the towns began to grow into cities.

Some of these stories will also serve to remind us that history is not always glorious or heroic. While many came from elsewhere to find success and happiness here, their fortune came at the expense of indigenous residents, like the Pauma or the Kupa, who found themselves reduced to tenants on their own lands, treated as virtual slaves or forcibly uprooted.

It's all history, the highs and the lows, to be preserved and remembered. Someone once said that every generation stands on the shoulders of the one that came before. Someone else once compared a nation ignorant of its history to amnesiacs, not able to remember who they are, where they came from or where they are going.

Scattered across San Diego County are historical societies, museums and libraries helping to preserve the history we all need to know. The paid staff and volunteers of these institutions, along with the employees of the San Diego County Parks and Recreation Department, have been an invaluable resource to me in digging out the history found in this book. I thank and salute them as too often unsung heroes, working to preserve the vital information telling us who we are, where we came from, and where we may need to go. I also express my gratitude to all for the permission they gave to use photographs from their archives. Their contact information appears at the end of this book. I urge readers to visit and support them.

Following that contact list is a resource list for readers who might want further information on the people, places or events covered in this book.

I also wish to thank my dear wife and business partner, Peggy Rossi, who did the editing and layout for this book. An accomplished graphic artist and genealogical researcher, she is also an incomparable life partner whose love of history and creativity inspired me to heights I could never have reached alone.

From Field to Town

Escondido

Lime Street School

Lime Street School circa 1890 *Pioneer Room/Escondido Public Library*

Two palm trees in Grape Day Park mark the site of what was once the Lime Street School. Completed in 1886, the school was one of the first buildings constructed in Escondido and was located on what was then the town's northern limit, by the banks of the Escondido Creek. The two-story, red brick structure was the city's first full-fledged grammar school, replacing the temporary Rock Springs School where first through ninth grades had been taught in one room.

The school was originally planned for 200 pupils but was soon "filled and overflowing," according to Frances Beven Ryan's 1970 book, *Early Days in Escondido.*

Howard Daley, of the Daley Ranch family, began attending the Lime Street School around 1892. The archives of the Escondido Library's Pioneer Room contain a file on the school which includes part of a manuscript written by Daley describing his time there.

"The school had four large classrooms and at the west end there were storage rooms the width of the building," wrote Daley. He recalled that corporal punishment was administered in the storerooms. "The creek back of the schoolhouse was full of willows, and the teacher made us go down and cut our own willows used for the whippings."

This was the period before Escondido had a separate high school building, and high school classes were held on the second floor, with elementary grades on the first. Daley recalled that "one day we had a severe earthquake. All the small children ran into the large hall at the same time. The big high school boys came spilling down the stairs, and it was a wonder the little children were not trampled."

During that same quake Howard Daley wrote that his older brother George Daley and friend James Cassou "jumped out a window, and our folks had to argue a lot to keep them from being expelled."

In 1894, the former Methodist Episcopal Seminary building was reopened as Escondido High School. That school was also used to take some of the overflow from Lime Street School. Sixth, seventh, and eighth graders "trudged up the hill to classes on the lower floor of the high school,"according to Ryan's *Early Days in Escondido.*

Even with the construction of a second grammar school in northeast Escondido in the early 1890s, the Lime Street School continued to operate above capacity. A September, 1907 *Escondido Times* article listed a total enrollment for that school year of 233.

The school building also functioned as a community center and in that capacity was the setting for one of the most significant moments in Escondido's history, the burning of the water bonds. On September 9, 1905, some 3,000 people gathered on the steps of the school to witness the burning of cancelled bonds from the old Escondido Irrigation District. The occasion was a city and countywide celebration of Escondido's "deliverance from the blighting debt," in the words of a contemporary *Escondido Times* article. For at least two years afterward, families would return would return to the school grounds each September 9 with picnic baskets to commemorate the event.

That bond-burning turned out to be Lime Street School's last hurrah. Evidence began to grow that the structure was being undermined by the sandy soil and the movement of the creek. In 1909 school staff expressed alarm over growing cracks in the walls, loosened keystones and bowed windows. School officials decided that a new building was necessary and the building was condemned and demolished.

Lime Street would be renamed Broadway and the site of the Lime Street School would become part of Grape Day Park.

The McFeron story

Many streets and roads in the city of Poway are named after pioneer settlers. McFeron Road, which runs east off Pomerado Road just north of Poway Road, is one such street. The McFerons settled in Poway in 1912 and lived there for four decades where they were ranchers and small business owners.

As is often the case with streets named after pioneers, McFeron Road is not located near the area where the McFeron family actually lived. The family is also honored by another road, Budwin Lane. That small road, which crosses Twin Peaks Road just west of Espola Road, honors Budwin McFeron, and it marks where his family moved after a period of adversity.

The McFeron story in Poway begins with Gershom "Gus" McFeron. Born in Missouri in 1859, Gershom headed west on the Oregon Trail, first settling in Washington. In 1909 he brought his family to San Diego and three years later he bought 600 acres in the Poway area, near what is now Route 67 heading up toward Ramona. The land, "which began as wilderness, was turned into a productive fruit farm," according to a 1993 article in the *San Diego Union-Tribune.*

A family photo pictured from 1918, now in the archives of the Poway Historical and Memorial Society, shows Gershom's son Budwin, then around 14, picking potatoes on the family ranch.

Asked about the photo, Jean Cook of Escondido, granddaughter of Gershom and daughter of Budwin, didn't recall the family growing

Budwin McFeron digging potatoes, 1918 — *Poway Historical and Memorial Society*

many potatoes other than for their immediate needs. "Peaches were the main thing."

Cook, 81, recalls stories of the family delivering their peaches over the Poway grade into San Diego to the city's farmers market in the 1910s and 1920s.

Farming could be a precarious business, even in good times. With the stock market crash of 1929 and the ensuing Great Depression, Gus McFeron lost his mortgaged farm. Budwin and wife Pauline managed to buy an abandoned house and 160 acres along what is now Budwin Lane.

Daisy Arlene McFeron, widow of Budwin McFeron, Jr., recalls how her in-laws, Budwin, Sr. and Pauline, were able to acquire the property: "They did without,"she said, scrimping and saving as best they could.

Once they'd moved in, with elderly parents to care for, they began taking in boarders to make ends meet. They had olive trees and raised hay and grain, but mainly for their own consumption, according to Jean Cook. "There wasn't any livelihood except for caretaking," she said.

Budwin Sr. and Pauline took in foster children. Caring for the elderly Gershom and his wife Nancy led them to decide to care for elderly people as well. They added on to their home, which became the McFeron Rest Home. In later years, under different owners, it would be known as Twin Peaks Retirement Home.

Budwin McFeron, Sr. worked at Convair's aircraft plant during World War Two, helping to build B-24 bombers, supplementing what the family made by operating the rest home. After the war, Budwin was weakened by heart problems, and wife Pauline became "chief cook, bottle washer and wage earner," according to Jean Cook.

Gershom McFeron died in 1945 at the age of 85. His wife Nancy died two years later. Budwin McFeron,Sr. died in 1958 at the age of 53. His wife Pauline lived to be 90, founding Valle Vista Convalescent Hospital and Crestview Manor, two facilities in Escondido.

The homesite on Budwin Lane was sold decades ago to developers. Today part of it is occupied by a subdivision, the other by an assisted care facility.

A tragic footnote was added to McFeron family history in 1978. James McFeron, brother of Budwin McPheron, Jr., was the pilot of Pacific Southwest Airlines Flight 182 when it collided with a small private plane and crashed in North Park, killing McFeron and 143 others.

Rancho Bernardo

Dining, dancing and fishing at Lake Hodges

The Lake Hodges Pavilion, circa 1940 *Pioneer Room/Escondido Public Library*

Before I-15, Rancho Bernardo and Escondido were connected by Inland Mission Road, which became State Route 77 in 1931 and was renamed Highway 395 in 1934. That road crossed Lake Hodges on a bridge erected in 1919. In the early 1920s a structure was built at the Rancho Bernardo entrance to the bridge that was first called the Lake Hodges Station Store, then the Lake Hodges Pavilion.

Nick and Shirley Buskirk, in their 1993 book, *Escondido: Then and Now*, refer to the pavilion as a popular dancing spot. "It was also a busy fishing camp with a boat dock, cabins and other facilities."

A front page article in Escondido's *Daily Times-Advocate* for May 20, 1924 announced a major remodeling of the station store that "would greatly enlarge the present dancing and dining rooms."

The article stated that "The dining room will face the lake and will be cooled by the breezes sweeping across the waters." The dance floor was to be expanded to hold "more than 200 couples." A "first class kitchen" was being added to offer chicken dinners "on Sundays, dance nights or by appointment" with "regular short order service" during the week.

The Saturday, June 7 *Daily Times-Advocate* carried a large, front-page ad announcing the grand opening of the new dance pavilion that night. An article on the same page noted that Lake Hodges had been stocked with 3,000 catfish and 100 bass the day before. Station store manager L. A. Hinshaw was said to be "jubilant over the prospects of having a great fishing resort at this station."

A five-piece jazz band from San Diego, "Jordan's Harmony Boys," provided the music on opening night at the pavilion. A local newspaper account the following Monday said dancing had begun at 9 p.m. "At midnight came a serpentine and confetti battle and the dances then continued until three o'clock. Manager Hinshaw was greatly pleased with the big success of his opening night."

In 1925 and 1926 ads appeared regularly in weekend editions of the *Daily Times-Advocate* announcing dance parties at the pavilion, according to historian Alan McGrew in his 1988 book, *Hidden Valley Heritage: Escondido's First 100 Years.*

In the mid-1920s Hinshaw was succeeded as manager by John Daley, who ran the pavilion until his death in 1943. In addition to the store, dance hall and lunch counter, the property included living quarters for the manager's family.

John Daley, Jr. lived in the house by the lake from the time he was born in 1928 until 1944, when his family moved to Los Angeles shortly after his father's death.

Daley said the property was owned by the City of San Diego. "My father was an employee of the City of San Diego Water Department."

"It was a great place to grow up," said Daley. "Highway 395 ran right across the front of our house and the lake was behind it. Traffic was nowhere near what it's like today."

Lake Hodges Station Store sometime in the 1920s *Pioneer Room/Escondido Public Library*

Daley remembered that while most of the dances in the 1930s were headlined by local bands, two Hawaiian bands would often appear as well. One that stood out in his memory was "Harry Owens and His Royal Hawaiians." Owens composed the popular hit, "Sweet Leilani." That song was inspired by Owens' daughter, who was then six years old, the same age as John Daley, Jr. when the band played at the pavilion. Daley remembers seeing her there.

Before his death in 2008, Bernardo Winery owner Ross Rizzo recalled riding a horse from the family winery down to Lake Hodges to visit his friend, Donald Blunt, whose father Herbert Blunt was the pavilion's manager in the late 1940s and early 1950s.

Rizzo was then too young to go to the dances, but with his friend being the manager's son, "we had the run of the whole place."

He remembered fishermen coming down from San Diego with their families and staying at the cabins. They would catch the fish and "pan fry them right out there" on the lakeshore. "The kids would pitch lines in the lake. The more people came the more kids there were, getting acquainted. It was good old family fun."

The area where the pavilion once stood was covered over when the freeway to San Diego was realigned in 1952. That spot now lies underneath the entrance ramp for I-15 off Pomerado Road.

The stars of Valley Center

If you were a child between 1951 and 1968 you may recall these words — "From out of the blue of the western sky comes Sky King!"They were the opening lines of a tv show that was a Saturday morning staple.

Sky King, the Flying Cowboy flew out of his Flying Crown ranch each week to do battle with various bad guys. In real life, Kirby Grant, the actor who played Sky King, was indeed a flier and a rancher, and until his death in 1985, his ranch was in Valley Center.

Just south of the intersection of Lake Wohlford Road and Valley Center Road is the remnant of an airstrip. This was Kirby Grant's private airstrip, according to Bob Lerner, historian with the Valley Center History Museum. Grant's home was at the end of the airstrip, fronting on Valley Center Road.

Grant was one of a number of film and television celebrities who called Valley Center home for at least some portion of their lives. Among those for whom the History Museum has documented a presence in Valley Center are Steve Reeves (*Hercules*), Ramon Novarro (the original *Ben Hur*), Gary Cooper, Jack Haley (Tin Man in *The Wizard of Oz*), Fred Astaire, Randolph Scott, June Allyson and husband Dick Powell, and Merle Oberon.

John Wayne had a home nearby in Pauma Valley, but his favorite riding trail was said to be an old stagecoach route through Valley Center, McNally Road between Cole Grade and Lilac Roads. Museum historian Lerner quotes a local newspaper item from 1940: "John Wayne and Loretta Young went riding Sunday last on McNally."

A lesser-known star who lived in Valley Center was Guinn T. "Big Boy" Williams. According to Bob Lerner, Williams's presence was not widely remembered until his former house was destroyed in the 2003 wildfires. Comments of neighbors and the memories of longtime residents led the museum to research his life. Information on Williams, who died in 1962, is now part of the museum's exhibit, "Cowboys To Crown Princes."

Williams got his nickname from his good friend, humorist Will Rogers, on the set of their first silent film together in 1919. "Big Boy" made 208 films over his 40-year career, most of them low-budget westerns. While he never became as famous as some of his contemporaries, Williams was successful financially and raised polo ponies on his Valley Center ranch.

Interesting stories about celebrities' interactions with their Valley Center neighbors can be found in a manuscript in the Valley Center History Museum's archives. It was submitted in 2004 by Helene Davidson, whose family, the Tanners, owned a store and café for many years on Valley Center Road. In the 1940s Davidson was a teenager who got "quite a thrill" coming into contact with the movie people.

One Sunday afternoon, when Davidson was working in the café, John Wayne came into town with his wife and another couple. Before they even entered the café, wrote Davidson, "you knew immediately it was John Wayne crossing the street." Wayne and his party ordered milk shakes. "No profit was made on his milk shake because I loaded it to the hilt with ice cream."

Wayne, described by Davidson as "cordial" and "very talkative," asked if "Randy," meaning Randolph Scott, "was home or not that weekend." Bob Lerner said that reference is the only documented case he's been able to find that "two of these celebrities knew each other." He has likewise yet to find any evidence of what brought so many show business people to the area.

"Of all the movie stars who lived in Valley Center, Randolph Scott was most intimately assimilated into the community," said Lerner. In her recollection of the World War II years, Helene Davidson wrote that Scott "attended Farm Bureau meetings held in the school hall and just rubbed shoulders more with the natives. He also worked shoulder-to-shoulder with his hired hands when he was present on the ranch. He raised pork and beef and grew hay or wheat."

Another Hollywood expatriate to Valley Center was Martin Gang, a lawyer and philanthropist whose list of clients included Jack Benny and Bette Davis. Lerner related an anecdote from the history museum's files passed on from Gang's children. Gang represented Bette Davis before the House Un-American Activities Committee in the early 1950s. In response to Gang's service, Davis jumped in her car one day and drove from Hollywood to Valley Center where she greeted Gang at his door by saying, "Thank you for saving my life." She then gave her lawyer a peck on the cheek, turned around, got back in her car and returned to Hollywood.

Lerner smiled and said, "Doesn't that sound like Bette Davis?"

The oldest Protestant church in Escondido

Escondido's First United Methodist Church officially celebrated its 121st birthday on November 11, 2007. "We're the oldest Protestant church in Escondido," said the Reverend Faith Conklin, Senior Pastor.

The church was incorporated as the Methodist Episcopal Church of Escondido in November, 1886. By the end of the following month the church had 19 members, according to a history prepared for the congregation's centennial in 1986.

As part of its efforts to promote development, the Escondido Land & Town Company offered free lots to any church wishing to establish itself in the new community. The Methodist-affiliated University of Southern California received 1,000 lots, valued at $100,000. The university sold the majority of the lots and used the proceeds to construct a church and a seminary. (The seminary would close in 1894 but its former headquarters would serve as Escondido High School until the late 1920s).

The Methodist Episcopal Church's first permanent home, at the corner of Grand and Ivy Streets, was dedicated on August 21, 1887. "The church is a handsome brick structure, with a seating capacity of about

Methodist Episcopal Church, circa 1890, with the USC Seminary in the background.
Pioneer Room/Escondido Public Library

250, and cost complete about $4,000," reported the *San Diego Union* at the time, as quoted in the centennial history.

First-hand memories of the original church building came from Harriett Church, 91, the longest-serving member of the congregation. Church is a former president of the Escondido Historical Society. She co-authored the 1986 centennial history and contributed to a 1996 booklet marking the 110th birthday. She began attending services at age five or six, she said.

One of her fondest childhood memories was ringing the church bell.

There were no stairs up to the steeple. A long rope hung from the bell's clapper down into the church entryway.

The 1996 church history said that Harriett "was swept off her feet as the bell's wheel and rope carried her a little way up. She held on and had no trouble getting back to the floor safely."

"I loved it," Church said.

Church also recalled people who came to services in horse-drawn carriages. They would tie up their horses to hitching rings at the curb, but in the course of the church service, "the horses would get restless, pull themselves away and go dancing down the street," she said. After the service, people would follow the sound of the meandering carriages to retrieve their rigs.

Nathan M. Wheeler was the congregation's first pastor at a time when the church existed only on paper, serving from May to August, 1886 before stepping down due to ill health. In his short tenure, he managed to build a parsonage, organize the congregation and start fundraising for the first church building.

Wheeler's successor, Amos Martin Ogburn, worked as a hod-carrier on the construction of the first church building. Ogburn was followed in October 1887 by John Neil Turrentine, who would go on following the end of his pastorate to serve Escondido in a number of civic capacities, including city clerk, postmaster, presiding officer of the local court, and newspaper editor-publisher.

As one of the few large buildings in early Escondido, the church also served as the site of non-religious community events. The centennial history noted that in early 1888 "the large crowds which had accompanied the celebration of the opening of the railroad to Escondido spilled over from the Escondido Hotel to be housed in the church and the

Rainey building, the city's only other large building. The following Memorial Day, the commemorative exercises were held at the church."

By 1920 the congregation had outgrown its church. A new Greek-style structure of cement blocks was built at the corner of Kalmia and Illinois (now Fourth) Streets and was dedicated in December 1921. The edifice at Grand and Ivy became a Lutheran Church and later a dance studio before being demolished in 1964.

In 1939, as a result of organizational mergers, the First Methodist Episcopal Church became the First Methodist Church. The congregation continued to expand, and by the mid-1950s the church complex included a social hall-education building and two parsonages.

In 1964 expansion necessitated the demolition of the old church and construction of a new edifice, which was built at the same Fourth and Kalmia site. In 1968 as the result of further mergers the First Methodist Church became the First United Methodist Church.

Bonsall

The little old schoolhouse

The Bonsall Union School District operates four schools today. However, if one refers to the "little old Bonsall Schoolhouse," most locals will know which one the person is talking about: the one story wood-frame building with the bell tower in front on Old River Road.

The 112-year-old building, near the school district offices and Bonsall Elementary School, is a remnant of Bonsall from before it was Bonsall. It opened in August 1895 as the Mount Fairview School, the community and the school district being called Mount Fairview at that time. Most of what's known about the building comes from the book, *The Little Old Bonsall Schoolhouse*, published in 1984 by the Landmarks and History Section of the Bonsall Woman's Club.

The schoolhouse as it appears today.
photo: Peggy Rossi

"The community surrounding the schoolhouse was one of large ranches and small farms," according to the book. "The hills were either dry-farmed for hay or dotted with cattle grazing."

The valley floor had a variety of farms, including dairies. vineyards, poultry and olive ranches, an ostrich farm, and several rabbit farms. There were also thoroughbred farms and apiaries. All water was obtained from the San Luis Rey River.

A drawing in the book depicts the little school along with a handful of other buildings clustered along the south bank of the river. The other buildings included a post office, blacksmith's shop "complete with tethering rock," a hotel and a general store.

The schoolhouse replaced an earlier Mount Fairview School, built around 1882. In the summer of 1891 a bond election to build a new school failed. However, another election in May 1894 resulted in passage, with all 21 district voters approving.

W. A. Stratton had donated land for a school site. In order to cut costs, community members volunteered to pick up lumber from the railroad and deliver it to the schoolsite. This was also done for the foundation stone, according to *The Little Old Bonsall Schoolhouse.*

Construction began in October, 1894. On August 26, 1895, the little school opened its doors to the first pupils. Elise Averill was the first teacher, hired at a salary of $60 per month. The school district also hired Nettie Dusing as a "janitoress," paying her $4.00 per month. The history compiled by the woman's club noted that "salaries had not increased since 1882 and, in fact, remained the same until 1905.... It would take 37 years (1882-1919) for a teacher to earn $90 per month, and the janitoress, $10.00."

The Little Old Bonsall Schoolhouse describes students walking to school or coming by buggy, knowing "class was about to begin when teacher stood in the doorway and rang the school bell." The preface lists among its sources of information old school records, microfilm of old newspapers, and conversations with "older area residents, former students."

The building served as a school until 1922, when the larger Bonsall Union School was dedicated. The little schoolhouse was moved to a location behind the new building. The Bonsall Union School was torn down in 1967 and replaced by the Bonsall Elementary School. In 1968 the little old schoolhouse was leased by the Bonsall Lions Club. The club moved the building to a site on the district grounds nearer to its original location. They also refurbished the building for use as a meeting place.

The Bonsall Union School District reassumed direct control over the building when the Bonsall Lions Club disbanded in 2004.

The historical research done by the Bonsall Women's Club won the schoolhouse designation as a county historic landmark in September 1990 by the Historic Site Board of the San Diego County Department of Planning and Land Use.

"They did very thorough research," said Elaine Davis, current chair of the Bonsall Woman's Club's Community Resources and Beautification Committee.

Camp Vista

The area of Vista off Sycamore Avenue that is today known as Green Oak Ranch was, from 1935 to 1941, the location of Camp Vista. The camp was one of a nationwide network of facilities created as part of the Civilian Conservation Corps. The corps, known more commonly as the CCC, was one of the first programs instituted by the administration of Franklin Roosevelt in the depths of the Great Depression.

The nation's economy was in desperate straits, with one-quarter of the workforce unemployed. CCC, which was originally aimed at unmarried males between 17 and 28, "brought together two wasted resources, the young men and the land," in the words of a capsule history on the website of the National Association of CCC Alumni.

Enrollees in "the triple C's" worked on projects including soil conservation, tree planting, preservation of wildlife habitat and road building.

When the program first got underway in 1933, the camps were very crude, with enrollees living in tents. By 1935, when Camp Vista was built, funding had improved. Camp Vista included four barracks, a mess hall, kitchen and bathhouse along with other buildings.

Camp Vista enrollees circa 1940 — *Vista Historical Society*

Articles in the *Vista Press*, obtained from the archives of the Vista Historical Society Museum, indicate that the camp at its maximum had 200 enrollees. Camp members were drawn from all across the nation as well as California.

Camp Vista opened in October 1935. That same month community residents organized the Vista Soil Conservation Association to coordinate conservation efforts with the CCC and other state and federal agencies. The *Vista Press* saluted these efforts in a November 1935 article, expressing hope that "a strong association membership can succeed in influencing the permanent maintenance of the CCC camp at Vista with all the worthwhile benefits of its continued effort on our conservation projects."

By March 1936, camp enrollees had constructed "47 permanent dams, over 4,500 feet of diversion ditches, one mile of terraces, and 70 permanent terrace outlet structures" on local ranches, according to a report by camp superintendent M. J. Carmody. This work was done "to demonstrate practical ways of controlling the washing of fertile soil from sloping lands," Carmody wrote.

During that same time "over 2,600 soil-holding, drought-resistant trees have been planted to protect gully banks and eroding hillsides," stated Carmody. Extensive programs for seeding and sodding, cleaning out and reconditioning flood control channels, and surveying were also well underway.

Enrollees were paid $30 a month. "That was a lot of money then," said Lauro Vega. Vega, who now lives in Chula Vista, joined the CCC in 1940 at the age of 17, serving six months at Camp Vista. Enrollees served for six-month periods. They could re-enlist, but Vega was able to secure a private-sector job with a farmer through his CCC service so he didn't have to rejoin.

For enrollees who were still part of their parents' households, Vega said $22 of their wages went directly to the parents, the rest to the enrollee. "It helped support our family," said Vega, adding that many CCCers supported families by working in the camps.

Vega's work at Camp Vista included fighting forest fires. "We fought fires all around Vista and Mount Palomar," he said. His other jobs included road building and soil conservation. He fondly recalls his time in CCC. "I learned how to work, how to take care of myself."

John Rubalcalva, 82, also served at Camp Vista in 1940. He said the daily routine was organized like the military, with enrollees awakened by reveille every morning and regular inspections of bunk areas and uniforms. The camp officers were drawn from the military reserves. Rubalcava called his time at Camp Vista "a very good experience" which prepared him for military service in World War Two.

Articles from the 1936 *Vista Press* state that Camp Vista also had an educational department offering instruction in radio, photography and drama. The camp also developed athletic teams as well as a band and glee club.

In 1939 an aeronautics course was begun which trained enrollees for jobs in the aircraft industry. In January 1940 a camp officer told the *Vista Press* that 28 of 44 students from the class had been hired by Ryan Aeronautical and Consolidated Aircraft to work in their San Diego facilities.

Mobilization for war began absorbing most of the unemployed workforce in 1940. Camp Vista closed in 1941 and the CCC program was discontinued in 1942. In 1984 the National Association of CCC Alumni placed a polished boulder with an inscribed plaque at the camp site, dedicated to the Camp Vista enrollees and the over 3 million young men who served in over 2,600 CCC camps throughout the nation.

The Escondido Hotel: A luxury destination

The Escondido Hotel stood from 1886 to 1925 on the hill now occupied by the Palomar Medical Center

Pioneer Room/Escondido Public Library

The City of Escondido didn't exist when the Escondido Hotel was completed early in 1886. Construction of the hotel by the Escondido Land and Town Company coincided with the company's hiring of a surveyor to plot townsite lots on the acreage formerly known as Rancho Rincon del Diablo.

A fine hotel to house prospective land buyers was a crucial part of the company's plan to develop a thriving community; real estate salesman were dispatched to lure land speculators and future homesteaders to visit.

The three-story, 100-room hotel was erected on a knoll looking down on what would become the east end of Grand Avenue. (The knoll is today the site of Palomar Hospital.) The first prospective land buyers arrived by stagecoach.

After the construction of the Santa Fe depot on the west end of Grand, the Escondido Hotel inaugurated a free shuttle service to and from the depot by horse-drawn, surrey-topped bus. The hotel and the railroad station became the anchors of a growing Grand Avenue shopping district.

The real estate boom in the new city meant a boom in business at the hotel. Within two years of the hotel's opening, 30 rooms were added.

The Escondido Times, which regularly reported arrivals at the hotel, noted that on a single day in 1888, 46 people checked in. They came from as far as New York City and Lansing, Michigan.

The hotel became a local landmark. (Called the Escondido Hotel prior to 1892, it was referred to subsequently as the Hotel Escondido.) *A History of California and an Extended History of Its Southern Coast Counties,* by J. M. Guinn, published in 1907, said the hotel was "recognized as one of the very best by its appointments of any in Southern California." Guinn described the building as commanding "on either side views of unsurpassed beauty."

The hotel sat within a 10-acre park "adorned with beautiful shrubbery and a large variety of ornamental trees, while its winding walks and driveways [were] made brilliant and fragrant by the many rows of exotic plants and native roses." A rose-covered veranda, extending almost entirely around the building, was, according to Guinn, "indicative of the comfort to be found therein."

The late local historian Frances Beven Ryan, in her 1970 book *Early Days in Escondido,* describes rooms "furnished with shiny brass knobbed beds, feather mattresses, snowy white sheets, patch work quilts and down pillows with stiffly starched, hand embroidered 'Goodnight' shams." In the spacious dining room beneath the elaborate lobby stairway, diners sat at tables covered with crisp white linen and set with polished silver. Each table also featured a vase of cut flowers and a basket of Escondido grapes.

For at least its first two decades, the hotel was a center of social life in Escondido. Prominent early settlers, such as Alvin Wohlford and William Pryor, were married there. Parties, as well as dances, drew people from throughout the region. The hotel's shuttle bus doubled as an excursion vehicle for "picnic parties,"and other local events.

While nationwide depression in the early 1890s put a dent in the local land boom, the hotel continued to be the prime spot for visitors and an area social center until 1915. That year the Panama-Pacific Exposition in Balboa Park spurred an influx in visitors that was felt throughout the county. The Hotel Escondido was booked to capacity. That year also saw the opening in Escondido of the Hotel Charlotta. The more modern Charlotta soon displaced the Escondido as the preferred hotel for visitors and as a gathering place for local citizens. The number of guests at the Escondido began a steady decline.

The Hotel Escondido closed its doors to guests in 1920, and in 1925 the building was demolished.

Fallbrook

Olive days

Before it was known for avocados and art, Fallbrook was a center of the olive industry. "The Olive Scores Again This Year and Demands First Place as a Money Crop in This District," proclaimed the headline of a January 1913 article in the *Fallbrook Enterprise*. The text of the article began by saying,"The olive seems determined to dethrone the citrus crop as king in this part of Southern California."

"During the period 1913-1915 olives were the largest cash crop in the Fallbrook area," wrote the late Don Rivers of the Fallbrook Historical Society in a 1998 essay, a copy of which can be found in the society's archives.

One of the first large cultivators of olives in Fallbrook was Dr. Charles Pratt. Pratt, an easterner by birth who came west for health reasons, began growing olives and lemons on his Loma Ranch around 1895, according to Rivers' essay. The ranch, which was located at the southern end of Alturas Street, had its own olive oil press and bottling plant producing "approximately 15,000 gallons of high-grade olive oil annually until 1919," wrote Rivers.

Another early center of olive production was the Red Mountain Ranch, which was located just northeast of Fallbrook at the top end of Live Oak Canyon. The ranch harvested 150 tons of olives in 1910, according to a March 1911 *Fallbrook Enterprise* article.

J. M. Cook, then superintendent of Red Mountain Ranch, authored a front-page article in the May 6, 1911, *Enterprise* in which he said Fallbrook's "granite soil is especially adapted to the peach, pear, lemon, orange and the olive." While noting the predominance of grain farming in the area for many years, Cook wrote that the grain farmer's place was " being rapidly taken by those who know the value of the soil for other purposes."

Olive groves and processing facilities proliferated in the Fallbrook area for a time. By early 1917 local growers had organized themselves as part of the California Associated Olive Growers. Under the auspices of the association a cannery was opened in March 1917 on Fallbrook Street between Main Avenue and Mission Road. The first shipment left the plant on March 5, 1917, 1,200 cases of 48 cans each, for a total of 57,600 cans, headed for New York, according to a contemporary newspaper article.

A 1978 *Fallbrook Enterprise* article recounted a 1920s banking deal in which an olive grower sought a loan from the Citizens Commercial Bank, then located on Alvarado and Main Streets. When the bank asked the grower for collateral, the grower said he had nothing to offer but olive oil. The bank lent the money after the grower "brought in a load of olive oil in five gallon tins which were stored on the bank floor." When the loan was repaid the man got his oil back.

As with other cash crops traded on the national and world markets, the olive was subject to steep fluctuations of demand. Contemporary newspaper accounts in the Fallbrook Historical Society show that within a year of the olive cannery's opening it was also processing tomatoes, spinach and other fruits and vegetables in addition to olives in order to remain profitable.

World War I led to an upsurge in demand for all kinds of produce, stimulating production in Fallbrook. However, the end of World War I also brought an end to tariffs on foreign olives and olive oil, resulting in a flood of imports from Italy, Greece and elsewhere which undercut local olive growers. A similar flood of olive imports would follow World War II, by which time the olive had been eclipsed in local prominence by citrus and avocados.

According to Don Rivers' 1998 essay, Red Mountain Ranch, under a succession of owners, was processing olives into the late 1970s. Today, other than individual souvenirs in private homes, Red Mountain olive oil bottles can only be seen as exhibits in the Fallbrook Historical Museum. Scattered groves of olive trees remain, along with street names like Olive Hill Road and Olive Avenue, as reminders of Fallbrook's olive days.

Red Mountain Ranch in 1892. The ranch was an early center of olive production in Fallbrook.
Barker-Kelsey Collection, Fallbrook Historical Society

Aerial view of the Prohoroff Poultry Farm, now the site of California State University, San Marcos. *San Marcos Historical Society*

San Marcos

An immigrant's dream

How many students and faculty members at California State University San Marcos campus today realize that the previous occupants of their campus were millions of chickens, residing on one of the largest chicken ranches in the world?

From 1945 to 1985 the Prohoroff Poultry Farm occupied 568 acres near Highway 78 and Twin Oaks Valley Road. It began as the dream of a poor immigrant family.

Terenty Prohoroff and his wife Mary came to the United States from Russia in 1907. They spent time in Texas, various parts of California and Arizona before settling for good in San Marcos in 1924. By that time, the family included four young children.

"When we came to San Marcos it was very sparsely populated, with just a house here and there," John Prohoroff, one of Terenty's four sons, told the *San Marcos Courier* in 1988. "It was still more or less wild country."

When John Prohoroff finished grammar school, Terenty wanted him to go to work to support the family. But John talked his father into letting him finish high school, reasoning that he could then take agriculture classes to help improve the family farm. His father agreed, although for years the ambitious young son would face much skepticism for his ideas on running the farm from his "old school" father.

"They were both fairly independent thinkers and each wanted their own way," said Kathy Shubin, granddaughter of Terenty and niece of John. "But John had a vision."

That vision started in 1945 with 250 chickens housed in one barn. It grew into what was for a time the biggest chicken ranch in the county and one of the largest of its kind in the world, according to a 1985 *Times-Advocate* article. At its peak the Prohoroff Poultry Farm housed some two million chickens on 557 acres, and produced over 328 million eggs annually.

An aerial photograph of the farm shows acres of white-roofed buildings. These, Shubin said, were the chicken houses where the laying hens were kept. Those houses made up the largest portion of the ranch which also had a separate section for young chicks, she said.

Shubin, whose father Jacob Shubin was a part of the family partnership running the farm, said her uncle John studied advanced methods for chicken raising. Among other things, "he developed a special formula for feed that would increase egg production."

A 1988 *San Marcos Courier* article noted that the Prohoroffs' operation "put San Marcos on the maps of farmers and agricultural departments from as far away as Australia and Japan."

The farm included a plant for processing fertilizer. Contemporary newspaper articles indicated the farm's operations generated almost 11 million pounds of chicken manure each month.

One of the customers for the Prohoroff's fertilizer was the Ecke family of Encinitas. Kathy Shubin recalled childhood memories of visits by Paul Ecke, Sr. to the farm, and of riding along with her father in a dump truck as he delivered fertilizer to the Eckes' plant-growing operation. Shubin also remembered that her family always got "hydrangeas at Easter and poinsettias at Christmas" from the Ecke family.

Shubin said she lived with her parents on the farm from infancy until the age of 19. The farm also included a dairy, and Shubin recalled that as a ten-year-old she had the job of milking cows and "picking up cow pies." She said she was often surprised when picking up what she thought was a cow pie to find instead it was one of the enormous local bullfrogs.

She refers to her childhood on the farm as "heaven on earth. Every child should be able to grow up like that, just being so close to nature."

Newspaper clippings in the archives of the San Marcos Historical Society show that the farm was down to around 100,000 chickens in the mid-1980s. In 1985 the Prohoroff family sold its land to three developers. Shortly thereafter the developers sold part of the acreage to the state of California for the construction of what is today the California State University San Marcos campus.

Kathy Shubin said that before his death in 1976 Terenty Prohoroff came to recognize the vision and accomplishments of his son John. John Prohoroff died in 1992.

While looking back with fondness on her farm days, Shubin said she was glad to see a university campus there now, and she thought her grandfather would feel the same way.

Patriarch of Palomar Mountain ranchers

The Mendenhall family has left its mark on Palomar Mountain, exemplified by the Mendenhall Valley. It was originally called the Malava Valley when Enos T. Mendenhall arrived on the mountain in 1869.

"Anyone entering for the first time one of the mountain's beautiful valleys, rich with grass, watered by a perennial stream, closed in by wooded hills, may imagine the effect on Enos T. Mendenhall when he rode into Malava Valley," wrote Marion Beckler in her 1958 book, *Palomar Mountain: Past and Present.*

Born in 1822 in North Carolina, Enos Mendenhall was descended from Quakers who had come to North America with William Penn in the 1600s, according to Arlie Bergman, Enos' great-grandson, who has researched the family's history.

While Mendenhall was still a young man, his family moved to Indiana, where he became a schoolteacher. In 1847, he pulled up stakes and joined a wagon train headed for Oregon. While in Oregon he met and married Rachel Emily Mills.

The young couple had a baby daughter in Oregon and soon came to California, first settling in San Francisco and then moving to the Sacramento area when the Gold Rush began. Eight more children were born to them, and six would live to adulthood.

Enos Mendenhall proved to be an entrepreneur, establishing a lumber mill and building three hotels, in Colfax, Sacramento and Grass Valley, according to Beckler's book. The site of his Colfax hotel, the Pioneer House, was marked with a commemorative plaque in 2007 by the city of Colfax as part of the city's annual Pioneer Day celebration.

While living in northern California, Mendenhall became acquainted with two men who would eventually become pioneer settlers in San Diego County, Alonzo Horton and Sam Striplin. It was at the behest of Horton and Striplin that Mendenhall came to southern California in 1869.

By some accounts he came on a secret mission as a lawman. Both Beckler in *Palomar Mountain: Past and Present* and Catherine Wood in her 1937 book, *Palomar: From Tepee to Telescope,* refer to Palomar Mountain as a haven for horse and cattle rustlers. Beckler describes Mendenhall as having "already proved himself" in "secret service" work with "Vigilantes Committees" in northern California. He is said to have established a pig ranching operation as a cover for gathering information on illegal activities on the mountain.

Enos Mendenhall
photo courtesy David Mendenhall

A family genealogy compiled by two of Mendenhall's descendants in 1961 states that Enos "aided the government in securing evidence towards conviction" of many wanted criminals who were living on the mountain.

Arlie Bergman said that while he has not been able to find corroborating documentation on Enos' law enforcement activities, he felt it was "very probable" that his great-grandfather had come south at Horton and Striplin's urging to gather information on rustling activities. He felt that the information Enos obtained stopped rustling operations there.

Whatever his original motivation, Enos was a serious rancher. "Seeing the possibilities of the mountain," wrote Catherine Wood, Enos sent for three of his sons then still living in northern California. "All took up claims when the land was thrown open for homesteading."

It was Enos's son Sylvester Jacob Mendenhall who led the transition from hogs to cattle raising, according to Arlie Bergman. Palomar Mountain's numerous meadow valleys "provide good summer feed for cattle," Bergman said. The problem, Bergman quickly added, came with the winter. "Two feet of snow is way too much for any kind of livestock to eat through."

In addition to acquiring land on Palomar, the Mendenhalls bought property at the foot of the mountain. The cattle would be driven down the mountain in the fall, then brought back up in March and April.

By the early part of the twentieth century, the Mendenhalls owned over 12,000 acres, and Sylvester Jacob Mendenhall had earned the nickname "Cattle King of Palomar Mountain." Enos Mendenhall died in 1904. Sylvester Jacob Mendenhall died in 1918. Descendants of Enos still live and work on and around Palomar Mountain today.

San Marcos

Silk and sunshine

Mulberry Drive got its name as part of a plan to make San Marcos a center of silk production. In the mid-1920s a group of businessmen purchased 367 acres of ranchland near what is now the intersection of Mission Road and Mulberry Drive. The area is just north of state Route 78 near California State University San Marcos.

On April 1, 1926, the group began planting the first of some 45,000 mulberry trees. mulberry tree leaves are the principle food supply of silkworms, which gorge themselves on the leaves, then spin cocoons from which raw silk is derived. In 1927, a 50,000 square-foot state of the art silk mill opened at the same location. A brochure put out at the time by the local chamber of commerce referred to San Marcos as "the valley of silk and sunshine."

During the previous decades there had been numerous unsuccessful attempts to develop an indigenous silk industry in California.

The San Marcos operation began as the idea of a northern California olive grower and nurseryman, Donly Gray, who grew and sold mulberry trees for shade out of his nursery near Marysville. After observing the heavy traffic in raw Asian silk headed to east coast ports on neighboring rail lines, he began to study silk production.

In an article written years later for the *Escondido Times-Advocate,* Gray described his dream of combining "a silk plantation, the cocoonery, the reeling plant, laboratories and the cloth spinning plant under one management and in the same locality, as well as housing for a professional staff and employees." The article was part of a retrospective series on the silk mill's 40th anniversary, copies of which are in the archives of the San Marcos Historical Society.

Needing backers, Gray joined with Glenn Hurst, a San Francisco businessman and promoter, who began recruiting other investors. After considering a number of sites in southern California, Hurst decided on San Marcos.

The company was chartered late in 1926 as American Silk Factors, Inc. Enough investors were attracted to create a nursery of almost 100,000 mulberry trees and a manufacturing facility that was the largest building in San Marcos at the time.

Glenn Gailey, who worked at the mill, described the operation in a 1984 interview with the *San Marcos Reporter*. Rows of mulberry trees were watered by a massive overhead irrigation system. The trees were kept short "so that reapers could come along and harvest the leaves for the worms."

Silk worm eggs were imported from Italy and France. "They came about 40,000 eggs to the box. We built a special incubator to hatch the eggs," said Gailey.

The hatched silk worms were then housed in thousands of trays, each six feet long and two feet wide, stacked 5 or 6 trays high. The worms were fed six times a day on chopped mulberry leaves.

Another silk mill worker mentioned the loud noise made by thousands of silk worms devouring the leaves. A website on the history of silk production (www.silk-road.com) compares the sound to "heavy rain falling on the roof."

Once the worms matured they would begin spinning their cocoons from which the fibers of silk would be then be separated and wound on to spools.

At its peak, the mill had 100 employees and by 1930 was producing some silk stockings. Production, however, never got beyond the experimental stage. The operation was at a disadvantage compared to lower-cost raw silk from Asia and Europe. The development of rayon as an alternative to silk around the same time, along with the 1929 stock market crash and ensuing depression, sealed the mill's fate. American Silk Factors declared bankruptcy in 1933 and the mill shut down. The operation was revived for 3 years in the mid-1930s by a new group of investors but that attempt also failed.

During World War II the government expressed an interest in reopening the mill to make silk bags for gunpowder. Donly Gray returned to the original site and found most of the mulberry trees dead. He estimated it would take at least three years to reactivate production which dissuaded the government from reviving the operation.

The mill building survives and today houses a sheet metal fabrication firm. An earlier remodeling in the 1980s turned up some old American Silk Factors correspondence along with some silkworm cocoons and raw silk. The items were donated to the San Marcos Historical Society where they are on permanent display.

Melancton Barnett: business man and civic leader

The name of Melancton Barnett does not appear in the annals of San Diego County history as often as those of his contemporaries like Ed Fletcher and William G. Henshaw. However, Barnett did business with both Fletcher and Henshaw and is said to have jousted with Fletcher in a land deal that preceded the construction of the Lake Hodges Dam.

Barnett descended from pioneering stock. His grandfather and namesake emigrated from New York state to the then-small village of Cleveland, Ohio in 1825, becoming a prominent businessman there, according to the 1914 book, *The Pioneer Families of Cleveland: 1796-1840*. Barnett's father, Augustus Barnett, left Ohio in the 1840s, heading west. He settled for a time in Wisconsin, where Melancton was born in 1857, then came to California in 1869.

The Barnetts first lived in San Jose, then moved to San Diego County in 1875. Two years later they moved to Ramona, where Augustus established the Barnett Ranch which would eventually grow to over 1,300 acres, producing beef and honey, among other products. Augustus was successful both as a rancher and as a financier. He also gave back to his adopted community, constructing a town hall in 1893 and deeding it in trust to the people of Ramona. Augustus Barnett died in 1906.

Barnett followed in his father's footsteps, both as a businessman and a civic leader.The archives of the Guy B. Woodward Museum in Ramona contain many of Barnett's financial records as well as some personal correspondence and other memorabilia that show his wide range of business and personal interests.

A 1916 state hunting license shows that Barnett, then 59 years old, was five-feet-eight-inches tall, had grey eyes and white hair.

Other documents show that in the late 1890s and early 1900s he was an active member of the San Diego County Fair Association and a trustee of the San Dieguito School District. A hand-written note from Evelyn Wile thanks Barnett for hiring her for the 1898 school year. There are also bills for school supplies addressed to Barnett, including a 1912 receipt for $3.85 from Loring and Company of San Diego for four textbooks.

Melancton Barnett owned "a lot of property in San Diego County," said Ken Woodward, Director of the Guy B. Woodward Museum. His holdings ranged from Del Mar to Ramona, and included 500 acres of the former Rancho San Bernardo. He was also apparently active as a broker mortgaging his own properties as well as others in a rapidly developing area.

Where today's Interstate 15 crosses Lake Hodges was Melancton Barnett's property in 1916. Ed Fletcher, acting on behalf of William Henshaw, was seeking land and financing to build what would become the Lake Hodges Dam and Reservoir.

Undated photo of Melancton Barnett (1857-1924)
Ramona Historical Society

In a January 1917 letter to Barnett, Fletcher offered a payment of $8,000 for "floodage rights" on 171 acres of his land. "It is entirely out of the question for us to buy all your property, for it runs into too much money," wrote Fletcher, assuring Barnett that he would "at all times...have absolute possession of the property...excepting when it is covered with water, which will probably be not to exceed three years out of twenty."

Fletcher urged Barnett to accept his proposition as "a service to the county," but also noted that getting financing for the dam project required first getting "some idea as to what it is going to cost. This is why we urge you to let us know at an early date if you will accept the $8000, or if you will arbitrate the damage or value of the floodage rights."

There's no copy of Melancton Barnett's response to Fletcher's letter, but other letters from Fletcher indicate that by November, 1917, the San Dieguito Mutual Water Company had agreed to acquire Barnett's floodage rights in exchange for paying off a $20,000 mortgage he had with the Southern Title Guarantee Company. This says something about Melancton Barnett as a negotiator.

Yet this shrewd businessman also used his $4,000 Locomobile to ferry high school football players from Ramona to games in San Diego, according to museum director Ken Woodward.

Melancton Barnett sold off most of his San Diego property holdings in the late teens before moving to Berkeley where he died in 1924.

The Community Church of Poway in 1916.

Poway Historical and Memorial Society

Poway

A lot of history in a little church

The little white church stands out today in a bustling neighborhood of homes, apartments and businesses in the heart of Poway. In photographs from Poway's rural past, however, the Community Church of Poway stands out as a lone building framed by meadows and distant hills.

In 1976 the Native Daughters of the Golden West, an organization of women who are direct descendants of pioneers, designated the church building as an historic site. An ornamental stone by the entrance bears a plaque that reads: "Community Church of Poway, United Church of Christ, founded by Methodist Episcopal Church 1883. Oldest structure in continuous use as a church in San Diego County. Erected circa 1887. Exchanged for Oceanside Congregational Church 1893."

Those four simple sentences encompass a great deal of history.

The church first opened its doors to worshippers in 1887 as the Poway Methodist Episcopal Church. Prior to that time, Methodist services had been conducted at the International Order of Good Templars Hall, according to Mary van Dam's 1985 book, *As I Remember Poway*.

In 1883 the Methodist Conference sent T. D. Lewis as Poway's first resident minister, spurring an upsurge in interest and support from pioneer residents. According to van Dam's book, Dr. Louis Hilleary donated several acres of land for the new minister to build a house and grow food.

Two other valley residents, Joseph and Amanda Stone, donated land for a church site at what is today the intersection of Community Road and Hilleary Place.

Volunteers supervised by Samuel Bowron erected the church, which was built of solid redwood, said Bob Good, longtime church member who has done research into church history.

Good, a retired naval pilot and operations research engineer in the aerospace industry, saluted the "really good workmanship" of the original builders.

The interior of the sanctuary is built in the shape of an inverted arc with the walls sloping inward to a flat ceiling. Two lanterns hanging from the center of the ceiling are original. Now wired for electricity, they originally used kerosene. The attic area between the flat interior ceiling and the peaked roof once housed a chain mechanism which was used to lower the lanterns to fill them with kerosene. Lamps mounted on the side walls are replicas, Good said.

An original steel rod stretches across the center of the sanctuary, connecting the two sloping walls at the level of the lanterns. Good praised this feature from an engineering point of view. "With all this weight coming down and this wide open space, that tension bar right there is what holds this building together," he said.

For its first few years, the Methodist church flourished. Van Dam's book described "well attended morning and evening services of worship, a large Sunday school and an enthusiastic Christian Endeavor group which met on Sunday evenings and was noted for its singing."

A severe drought in the early 1890s drove many residents out of the Poway Valley, leaving "a weakened church,"van Dam wrote.

Methodist church officials in Oceanside, who were numerically strong but had no church building, approached local members of the Congregational Church, who had a building but few members, proposing an exchange of properties between the Poway and Oceanside churches. This was agreed to, and in 1893 Henry C. Abernathy was appointed the first resident minister for Poway's Congregational Church community.

In the 1920s the name was officially changed to the Community Church of Poway. In the ensuing decades there were some hard times. There were years when the resident minister's position went unfilled, but lay members kept the church alive by conducting services and teaching Sunday school.

According to a 1963 church history compiled by Mrs. Forest Paulson, the church briefly closed its doors in 1949. But "a few of the older valley residents sought the help of the Congregational Conference in Los Angeles," which helped lead a reorganization.

In 1957 the Community Church became part of the United Church of Christ.

A revitalized church celebrated its 100th anniversary in 1987, starting construction of a new sanctuary and fellowship hall.

The historic original sanctuary has been preserved and is used for services twice a year, at Christmas and Easter, according to Bob Good. The building is also available by appointment for weddings, memorial services and other special events. Good stressed that the church is open to all. "We have a bit of pride in being the *community* church."

You knew you were home when you saw the tepee

For almost five decades—from 1929 until 1977—the tepee was a major landmark in Escondido. The giant wigwam-shaped structure was made out of wooden boards covered with tar paper, reinforced by three steel rings. Resting on an enormous concrete slab, the tepee stood 50 feet high and 60 feet in diameter.

Perched on a 960-foot hill between San Pasqual Valley Road and Summit Drive, the tepee was visible for miles around. Aircraft pilots used it as a location point. "You knew you were home when you rounded the hill and saw the tepee," is a phrase often repeated even today by longtime Escondido residents.

The tepee was constructed in 1929 by A. L. Houghtelin who was known alternately as Abraham or sometimes Abram according to accounts in the *Escondido Times-Advocate.* Then almost 60, Houghtelin was an Idaho rancher who purchased acreage on and around the hill and planted avocado and citrus. He also terraced the hilltop with retaining walls topped by slabs, all made out of poured concrete. The wooden forms used to mold the concrete ultimately went into construction of the tepee.

Over the years, Houghtelin and his sons gave varying explanations for what they'd planned, ranging from a residence for Hougthtelin's retirement to a guest lodge to a "come-on" for drawing real estate investors.

Whatever plans Houghtelin had were cut short by the Great Depression. A.L. returned to Idaho with his son John. His other son Clair Houghtelin stayed behind to continue ranching in Escondido. A. L. Houghtelin died in 1956.

While no further development was ever done on the tepee, it was to become a sort of unofficial community attraction and gathering place.

One night in the summer of 1939, the interior of the tepee became a ballroom for a party thrown by college students Connie Johnson and Murray Ehmke, according to stories published in the *San Diego Union* and the *Times-Advocate.* "Li'l Abner" was the theme of the party, which included livestock, willow tree cuttings and a live orchestra. Cornmeal was thrown on the rough concrete floor to allow comfortable dancing.

During World War II the tepee was used by civil defense spotters looking for unidentified aircraft.

Over the years, the tepee hosted many other formal activities including hayrides, Boy Scout and YMCA gatherings and meetings of the Escondido Historical Society. The tepee remained the private property of the Houghtelin family which authorized the use of the site for such activities.

The tepee also served as a gathering point for more "informal" activities for young Escondidans who would sneak on to the site for parties, romantic rendezvous or just to get away for a while.

The tepee's location, its unusual design and unfinished infrastructure gave it a special effect. The hilltop site with its giant concrete-walled squares and circles struck many visitors as a mysterious ruin. The tepee's cavernous interior, with its sloping walls slanting upward and inward to a tiny hole open to the sky, could appear magical. The view through any of the three doors, up to 50 miles on a clear day or night, added to the charm.

Going up to the tepee became a ritual for several generations of young people. "All our boyfriends would take us up to the tepee," recalls longtime Escondido resident Suzanne Hinrichs. "A wonderful view, and mystery, all that concrete."

"My husband took me up there in our '36 Ford. That was 1944," remembers Virginia Thomas.

Property owner Clair Houghtelin tolerated such informal visits to the tepee for many years. But by the mid-1960s, vandalism was becoming more of a problem as well as destruction of crops by trespassers.

Possible purchase of the tepee by the county or by other developers, discussed in a 1957 *Daily Times-Advocate* article, never came to fruition. By 1976, concerned about the weakening of the aging structure as well as continuing vandalism, Houghtelin blocked off the driveway leading to the tepee.

In May, 1977, Houghtelin was quoted as saying, "It isn't safe for visitors to go up there. Boards tear off it, and it might even topple in a high wind."

The fear of toppling came true eight months later. On December 20, 1977, exceptionally strong Santa Ana winds caused the big wigwam to collapse into rubble.

Castle in the canyon

In the midst of the boulders, oak trees and cactus of Moosa Canyon stands the tower of a medieval castle, three stories high with turreted top and walls three feet thick. It has stood there for 115 years, lending its name to Old Castle Road, which runs nearby.

Undated photo of Woreland Castle, built by Issac Frazee near what is now Old Castle Road.

Pioneer Room/Escondido Public Library

The building originated in the convergence of a bloody Old West gun battle and a gentle artist with a dream.

The gun battle was a January 1888 shootout in the canyon that left four people dead. The artist was Isaac Jenkinson Frazee, called in by the sheriff's office to sketch the crime scene.

Born in Indiana in 1858, Frazee moved with his family to southern California in 1873, according to Craig Walker, his great-grandson, who has extensively researched Isaac Frazee's life.

When he went to Moosa Canyon in 1888, Frazee was homesteading a ranch in the San Luis Rey Valley while also painting and writing poetry. Coming to do the sketches, Frazee fell in love with the canyon. Trees and a nearby waterfall touched his artistic sense. Indian artifacts found on his wanderings heightened his longtime interest in American Indian culture.

He went back and convinced his reluctant wife Bettie to pull up stakes and sell the homestead. He used the money from the sale to buy 160 acres in Moosa Canyon. The Frazees arrived there in 1890.

Isaac Frazee "was a dreamer," said Walker. "That was part of the reason he built the castle." Frazee had traced his ancestry back to inhabitants of Dunnotar Castle near Aberdeen, Scotland and sketched a blueprint for a castle home modeled after Dunnotar.

For two years Frazee worked on his own, breaking up rocks to be used to build his castle. He and his wife lived in a tent at first and later in a wooden house erected nearby. One day a man named Donald McGilvriap came passing through and asked for a drink of water. Finding out that McGilvriap was a Scottish stone mason, Frazee hired him.

By 1893 Frazee and McGilvriap had built the tower and part of an adjoining outer wall. Then the stonemason had to leave and Frazee ran out of money. "So he moved his two-story wood-framed house next to the tower and called it good," said Walker.

Frazee originally called his castle Warland in acknowledgement of the gunfight. He subsequently altered the name to Woreland Castle. The Frazees raised seven children at the castle, instilling in them a love of nature and the arts.

Often Frazee would decide to keep a painting he'd just finished rather than sell it or give paintings away to friends. Frazee spent hours developing the property as a park, inviting people from all over the area to come and camp there, but he never charged admission.

The Frazees presided over an informal colony of artists and intellectuals. In addition, they put on musical pageants with family and friends at a natural amphitheater on their property. The "Peace Pipe Pageant," staged in 1915, attracted 1,500 people from all over the state, according to an article in the August 23, 1915 *San Diego Union*. Participants included Ellen Beach Yaw, a prominent singer of the day who was a family friend. Music was written by another friend, W.M. Bower, a member of the Los Angeles Symphony Orchestra.

The pageant was written up in *Sunset Magazine*, which called it "one of the most remarkable outdoor pageants" in the state's history. Again, no admission was charged. To Frazee, "the essence of love was service," said Walker.

In the early 1920s advancing age made it more difficult for Isaac and Bettie Frazee to maintain their relatively isolated estate. The accidental death during the same period of their oldest son Jenkinson was a further blow. In 1922 the Frazees began spending the winters in Laguna Beach, returning to their castle home in the summer months. In 1927 they moved permanently to Laguna Beach. Isaac Frazee died in 1942.

The old castle, with additional rooms added, has continued as a private residence for a number of owners over the decades.

The town of Barham

Before there was a town of San Marcos in the San Marcos Valley there was the town of Barham. It was founded in 1883 by John H. Barham and his father James Barham. The town was located at the southeast corner of what is now San Marcos Blvd. and Rancho Santa Fe Road.

Local historian William Carroll, in his 1975 book, *San Marcos: A Brief History*, wrote that the town covered 640 acres.

A post office opened in 1883. By 1884, according to Carroll's book, "Barham boasted a blacksmith shop, feed store, and a weekly newspaper." John H. Barham operated a farm, ran the feed store and helped develop the town. His father James, who had a homestead, also served for a time as an overseer of the local road district for San Diego County.

The town of Barham opened the first school in the San Marcos Valley in 1886.

Another town leader was William Webster Borden. In 1884, he founded a weekly newspaper called *Our Paper*, which subsequently became *The Plain Truth*. Published every Saturday from "Barham, San Diego Co., California," Borden's paper combined local and countywide news and gossip with religious instruction and a little humor.

In an August, 1884 item, Borden explained to readers that he'd received a letter from a reader he referred to as "Kus-T-Mur, which with all respect to the writer, we cannot conscientiously publish, as our salary is limited and we do not feel justified in employing a bodyguard..."

John H. Barham with wife Olley and son Thomas in 1911.
San Marcos Historical Society

An issue early in the newspaper's first year enthused that Barham was "on the boom," reporting that "Mr. John Schmaker of Los Angeles (a carpenter by trade) has put up a house, plowed land and planted some crop since the first of May." The article went on to report the coming of two other new residents who had done the same.

Making a living, however, was difficult, with water scarce and transportation limited to a few wagon roads. Two months after writing about the "boom" in Barham, *Our Paper* noted "The past season has been a very severe lesson...especially to those who depend entirely to the raising of wheat for a livelihood. It has taught them, at great cost, that wheat alone will not due to depend on." The article went on to advocate balancing of various grains along with the raising of poultry and livestock, and cultivating orchards.

The fortunes of town founder and namesake John Barham appeared to fluctuate. An item in the February 9, 1884 *San Diego Union* reported that Barham "desires to sell his stock of goods and rent his building." Just two weeks later, however, the *Union* announced that "Johnny Barham has changed his mind in regard to selling out; he has laid in a $2,000 stock of goods and believes that 'opposition is the life of trade' and will sell 'cheap, for cash.'"

By April of 1884, the *Union* was reporting that John Barham had enlarged his store and was making arrangements to put up a "steam flouring mill" and a "whiskey mill." In July of that year the paper noted that Barham had "20 big stacks of grain and will commence threshing next week."

Over the next few years, however, the fortunes of Barham and his town were to fade. John Barham sold his land and his store in 1887 and left San Diego County. In a 1980 oral history interview for the San Marcos Historical Society, Barham's son Thomas said his father "sold out due to the general dry weather conditions in the area."

Another factor affecting Barham's fate involved the coming of the railroad which had been much anticipated by residents in the San Marcos Valley. When it arrived in early 1888, the line ran two miles north of Barham, much closer to a townsite set up in 1887 by the San Marcos Development Company. This site became a stronger attraction for investors and new settlers than Barham.

Early in 1888 William Webster Borden, who served as postmaster, closed down the town's post office. In December 1888 Borden changed the mailing address of his newspaper from Barham to San Marcos. In 1889 the Barham schoolhouse was moved to the San Marcos townsite. Borden himself would later move to Carlsbad.

The town of Barham faded into history. Today two streets in the City of San Marcos, named Barham and Borden, are all that remain to recall the early settlement.

Warner Springs

The Cupeño expulsion

The area known today as Warner Springs Ranch was originally called Kupa, after the indigenous people who first settled it. Known today as the Cupeños, they came to the region 800 to 1,000 years ago. They lived there in relative isolation and peace until 1795 when the first whites came to their valley.

The valley's location at the headwaters of the San Luis Rey River and its possession of natural springs made it "a natural way station on any route from the south or east through the Arizona desert to the coast of California," according to *Introduction to the Cupeño People*, published by the Cupeño Cultural Center.

The original Mexican land grant for the region was bestowed "without prejudice to the indigenes [native peoples]." The original grantee, Jose Antonio Pico, failed as a rancher and in 1844 the property was granted to Juan Jose Warner.

Warner's land grant didn't mention the Indians at all according to a 1973 history of the Cupeños, *Mulu'wetam: The First People*, by Jane Hill and Rosinda Nolasquez. The grant described the land as "vacant and abandoned," evidently in a reference to the buildings which had been built by the Indians under the supervision of Franciscan fathers from Mission San Luis Rey.

That description of vacant land flies in the face of other contemporary accounts of lands under cultivation for grain and vineyards or of cattle being herded, with much if not all of the work being done by Indians.

In 1846 General Kearney's army unit passed through the ranch on the expedition that would lead to the Battle of San Pasqual. Dr. John Griffin, an army doctor, wrote in his journal of how hard the ranch Indians worked but also described their treatment by Warner as "worse by far than the worst treated slaves in the United States." Another of Kearney's officers, Captain A. R. Johnston, wrote in his journal that the Indians "are stimulated to work by $3 a month and repeated floggings."

California's becoming part of the United States brought no relief to the oppressive conditions suffered by the Cupeños. In fact, they were further humiliated by the imposition of taxes on their land and cattle, leading in 1851 to the Garra Uprising, named for its leader, Cupa chief

Antonio Garra. Warner's ranch buildings were burned down and nine Americans were killed before the revolt was put down by U.S. Army troops. Garra and William Marshall, a white sailor who aided the uprising, were executed.

Warner moved to Los Angeles after the revolt, running the ranch through intermediaries. It appears the rebellion did win the Cupeños some rights over the ranch's hot springs. In an 1867 letter to a prospective buyer of the property, Judge Benjamin Hayes noted that on a recent visit, the Indians "seemed to regard the immediate vicinity of the spring as their own. I paid them a dollar for my bath, at the rustic bathing establishment they have constructed..."

Cupeños Trail of Tears, a 2003 commemorative history compiled by the group E Clampus Vitus, noted that by the late 1880s, the Cupeños were totally self-supporting through farming and operations of a hot springs resort.

The commercial potential of the hot springs proved irresistible to John G. Downey, a former governor of California who had purchased Warner Springs Ranch in 1880. In 1892 he filed a complaint in the Superior Court of San Diego County to have the Cupeños evicted from the ranch. It was the beginning of a legal battle that would go on for over a decade, culminating in a 1901 U. S. Supreme Court decision against the Indians.

An offer was made to purchase the property from the Downey estate but the asking price was too exorbitant for the Cupeños and their supporters to meet.

On May 12, 1903, Indian Bureau agent James Jenkins arrived with 44 armed teamsters to carry out the eviction. Rosinda Nolasquez, a Cupeño who was 11 years old at the time of the eviction, described it years later in *Mulu'wetam.* "Many carts stood there by the door. People came from La Mesa, from Santa Ysabel, from Wilakal, from San Ignacio —came to see their relatives. They cried a lot. And they just threw our belongings, our clothes, into the carts, chairs, cups, plates. They piled everything on the carts." The government had ordered the Cupeños to be relocated to the Pala Reservation, forty miles away. The trip took 3 days.

The Cupeño became part of the Pala Band of Mission Indians. But the relocation was never forgotten. On the 100th anniversary of the eviction in May, 2003, the Pala Band rented a portion of the Warner Springs Resort to allow the descendants of the evictees to return and commemorate the loss of their homeland and celebrate their survival as a people. The commemoration has become an annual tradition.

A 1912 view of the home of Martin Fjeld. On the porch are (l. to r.) Elmer Fjeld, his sister Dora, Martin Fjeld and his wife Annie. *Pioneer Room/Escondido Public Library*

Escondido

Elmer Field: a skilled mechanic

When Elmer Field passed away in 1995 at the age of 94, his brief obituary in Escondido's *Times Advocate* stated that he was self-employed as a rancher and machinist.

Elmer Field's family operated a ranch at the intersection of Citrus Avenue and Glenridge Road for much of the 20th century. Photographs and transcripts detailing his life can be found today in the archives of the Escondido Public Library's Pioneer Room.

Elmer was born in 1901 in Iowa to Martin and Annie Fjeld , descendants of Norwegian immigrants. Elmer changed the spelling of his surname from Fjeld to Field decades later.

Martin Fjeld farmed 80 acres in Iowa, but was restless to "go West." He took his family to Colorado and then Idaho where a daughter, Dora, was born in 1906. The Fjelds ran a successful ranch in Idaho. Materials in the Pioneer Room reveal that Martin Fjeld also showed an aptitude for machinery. He built a grain mill with a steam boiler and other equipment.

Concerned by Martin's chronic respiratory problems and the lack of churches in the community for her children's religious education, Annie Fjeld wrote for brochures from communities in southern California.

The Fjelds relocated to Escondido in 1910. In 1911, Martin bought a six-room house and 13 acres of land on Citrus Avenue from W.H. Wilson. He built a barn, a machine shop and sheds for poultry. He planted grapes, berries and orange trees, and gradually acquired more acreage, including ten acres on the northwest corner of Glenridge and Citrus where he planted lemon trees.

Martin's son Elmer and daughter Dora helped their parents on the ranch while attending Orange Glen School. In oral history interviews with Ruth Collings of the Escondido Historical Society from the late 1980s , Elmer described delivering fresh milk and his mother's home-made butter to local customers as a child. After completing the eighth grade he left school to work full time on the ranch.

At that point agriculture was becoming more mechanized and cars were replacing the horse and buggy.

Elmer inherited his father's mechanical aptitude. Father and son learned how to keep all their farm machinery and cars in good repair in their own machine shop.

Word of their skills with machinery spread and around 1918 they began doing maintenance work for others. As Elmer told an oral history interviewer in 1984, "If somebody brought a Model T in to overhaul on Monday morning, I'd have it done for them at the end of the week. I did the complete engine, furnishing the parts, labor and everything for eighty dollars. And I was getting rich at eighty dollars."

All the business was by word of mouth, but Elmer soon had a three-month waiting list of customers for engine overhauls.

In 1925 Elmer married Martha Meyer, a German immigrant. He built a house on the corner across from his parents' home, farming the ten-acre lemon grove. He and Martha lived there for 47 years, raising two daughters, Norma Adele and Irma Ann.

Norma Field Bussey, 77, remembered that her father "did a lot of work for Churchill and Cassou [a longtime Escondido hardware and appliance store] making well pumps." She recalled running errands to get parts for him for jobs he'd be working on. She also recalled how hard her mother worked on the ranch.

During World War II, Elmer worked as a machinist at the North Island Naval Air Station. This was also when he changed the spelling of his surname from Fjeld to Field, telling historical society interviewers years later that "I didn't want to have to keep explaining that it was 'j', not 'i.'" He returned to the ranch in 1946.

Elmer's father Martin Fjeld died in 1965 just six weeks short of his 90th birthday. Annie Fjeld died in 1979 at the age of 100. Elmer's sister Dora, who had been a schoolteacher, died at 73 in 1980.

In 1972 Elmer and Martha Field sold their ten-acre grove to a developer and moved to a house on a quarter-acre of the original family property. Martha Field died in 1984.

In 1985 Elmer sold part of the remaining family acreage to the city of Escondido. That acreage became Mountain View Park. Norma Field Bussey said that people were still coming to her father's machine shop for custom lathe work in 1989 when he was 88 years old.

He continued working in the shop until about six weeks before he died in 1995, she said.

Elmer Field's last house is now a private residence. His parents' house still stands, boarded up, along with the corrugated metal building that housed the machine shop. They are owned by the City of Escondido which hopes to restore them.

Sickler Brothers Mill

Just off Highway 76 in Pala, at the northern-most edge of San Diego County, sits the Wilderness Gardens Open Space Preserve. In the midst of this county-run park stands the rock foundation of a building with a large, cast-iron wheel sitting alongside.

This structure is the remnant of the Sickler Brothers Mill. The mill, which existed from 1881 until around 1890, was the first and for many years the only gristmill in northern San Diego County.

Old photographs show that the foundation supported a three-story wooden building. The water wheel was located on the east side of the structure.

The Sickler Mill "exemplifies the ranching and homesteading period of the late nineteenth century in northern San Diego County," according to a report published by the county's Department of Parks and Recreation. The report, prepared by San Diego County Historian Lynne Newell Christenson and researcher Ellen Sweet, led to the designation of the structure as a county historic site in September 2005.

Gristmills, or flour mills, were places where farmers brought their crops of wheat, corn or barley to be ground into flour. "Mills were essential to a farmer's economic success," writes Christenson, with farmers needing a large mill to grind and bag their grain for sale.

In 1881 brothers William A. and Marion M. Sickler bought land along the San Luis Rey River and began building a mill. Up to that point William had worked as a schoolteacher while Marion had been a surveyor.

The brothers were serious about their business. Two large grinding stones, built in France, were shipped from Missouri—where the Sickler family had formerly lived and operated a mill—to Oceanside and then hauled to Pala by wagon.

The mill building stood about 30 feet tall. For the time period "that's a pretty noteworthy building," said Jake Enriquez, District Manager for the county parks and recreation department.

Pointing out details from old photographs of the mill, Enriquez noted that each of the building's windows was made up of twelve panes of glass. Given the cost of glass, milled wood, and other details, "it's clear the Sicklers were very serious about their investment in the mill," he said.

The cast-iron water wheel, which survives, was built in San Francisco to specifications set down by the brothers. Just under 6 feet in diameter, its surface is studded with large buckets or paddles.

The Sicklers built a flume to divert river water, carrying it down a twenty foot drop to the mill, where the force of the water drove the wheel which turned a shaft that moved the grinding stones.

The mill opened for business in November, 1881. The county historian's report, citing articles in the *San Diego Union* from that period, noted that by December, 1881 "the mill had all the work it could handle, turning out 12 barrels of flour per day."

The processing of the crops was a time-consuming business. Since it was the only mill in the area and the only means of getting the crops to the mill was by horse-drawn wagon, "it often took people several days to get to and from the mill," and once there "people had to wait from several days to several weeks to get their crop processed."

The mill became a community gathering place. "Customers and their families would camp at the mill for two weeks or more, sharing stories and recipes, and trading goods."

The mill owners created a makeshift school to teach children whose families were camped out on the mill grounds.

The mill operated successfully for about a decade. Then as railroads became more developed in the county, it became easier and cheaper for farmers to send their crops by train to be stored and processed in Los Angeles and elsewhere. As transportation patterns changed, the Sickler Brothers Mill was "out of the loop," according to Enriquez.

The brothers moved on to other business ventures. Under other owners, the mill complex evolved into a hunting retreat and later was part of a horticultural venture before becoming part of Wilderness Gardens Preserve in 1973.

The county is continuing its research into the mill's history, and invites the public to visit the mill site as well as the rest of Wilderness Gardens Preserve. The park is located at 14209 Highway 76.

This photo, taken in 1925, shows workers constructing the Vista Flume which eventually carried water from Lake Henshaw to Vista. *Vista Historical Society*

Vista

Water made the difference

Vista's first water supply was the Buena Vista Creek. Its first well was at Rancho Buena Vista, the 1845 Spanish land grant whose acreage would be developed in the late 1880s to form the community that became Vista.

The 1983 book, *A History of Vista,* by Harrison and Ruth Doyle reported that first Vista Water Company was organized in 1911. The company furnished water to users from a series of wells along Buena Vista Creek for almost two decades.

"In those early days agriculture was limited to cattle grazing and dry farming, with the exception of the small areas along the creeks and a couple of vineyards," wrote the Doyles.

Community residents recognized the limitations of shallow local wells and the need for a better irrigation system. In the summer of 1923 local residents petitioned the county board of supervisors to form an irrigation district in accordance with the provisions of the state Irrigation District Act.

The board of supervisors granted the petition on July 19 and called for a special election the following month. On August 14, 1923, residents voted 104 to 4 in favor of creating the Vista Irrigation District. Voter turnout was 100 percent.

The members of the first elected district board were George S. Henry, Jules Delpy, F. J. Knight, H.S. Merriam, and Chester D. Gunn. The new board met on September 18, 1923 and initiated negotiations with the San

Diego County Water Company and the Escondido Mutual Water Company to access water from Lake Henshaw. The board also had to work out district boundaries and the water rights of individual users.

In October, 1924, with all the necessary legal agreements having been reached, an election was called to approve $1.7 million in bonds to construct the irrigation system. District voters approved the bonds by a vote of 96 to 0. An article in the May 7, 1925 *Oceanside Blade* reported Vista Irrigation District's approval of contracts "for approximately 60 miles of concrete pipe lines," described as "the largest cement pipe job in Southern California" at that time.

At a large celebration on May 16, 1925, ground was broken for the Vista Flume. Throughout that spring and summer, work progressed on the flume and various components of the system, including a dam and five circular concrete reservoirs.

Enough of the system was completed for Vista to celebrate the arrival of the first water from Lake Henshaw on February 27, 1926.

"Vista is Host to Thousands At Opening of Irrigation District," proclaimed a headline in the *Oceanside Blade*. "The town was in gala array with flags and bunting," the *Blade* reported, "while elaborate decorations marked the stands that had been erected for the distinguished guests and outlined the course that had been laid out for the presentation of an historical pageant and the rodeo events and other sports that followed." A parade included floats representing Spanish mission days, a U. S. Marine band, and decorated automobiles carrying district and state officials, representatives from the clergy and Indian communities at the San Luis Rey Mission and rodeo contestants.

After a number of speeches State Senator Ed Sample, representing the governor, pressed a button which turned on the water amid enthusiastic cheers.

The coming of water was indeed a milestone event for Vista. An article in the February 17, 1928 *Vista Press* cited figures from irrigation district officials who "conservatively estimated that there are now 1,200 persons residing in the district." By contrast, in February 1926, when the irrigation system first started delivering water, "there were less than 350."

Hay, grains and other dryland crops gave way to tomatoes, citrus and avocados. By the mid-1940s, the Vista area was known as the Avocado Capital of the World. The water had made all the difference.

Fallbrook's lost landmark

For nearly 70 years the most prominent landmark in Fallbrook was a hotel which occupied a square block between Alvarado and Fig Streets. Between its opening in 1889 and its demolition in 1958, the hotel would go under three different names, but the graceful Victorian structure would be instantly recognizable to residents and visitors alike.

Pictures of the long-gone hotel show what must have been a quite striking building. The three-story wooden structure had 52 rooms, a redwood-shingled roof and a two-story cupola that invited comparisons with the Hotel Del Coronado, which was built during the same period. A veranda wound around the front of the building's first floor.

The building first opened for business in 1889 as the Francis E. Willard Hotel, named for the then-national president of the Women's Christian Temperance Union (WCTU). According to research done by the Fallbrook Historical Society, Francis W. and Mary Bartlett, co-owners of the land on which the new hotel stood, were strong supporters of the WCTU. They were not alone among Fallbrook residents in their sentiments.

In 1897 the hotel was leased by George and Laura Westfall who renamed it the Naples Hotel. Years later, their son Victor Westfall, in a reminiscence published in the *Fallbrook Enterprise,* talked of the hotel's popularity: "Drummers—that's what we used to call traveling salesmen—used to hurry their business in Temecula so they could come to Fallbrook, spend the night, and enjoy my mother's cooking. Families from San Diego used to come up for weekends. They got supper with wild duck or quail as an entrée, a room for the night, and breakfast."

In 1911 William Ellis, a prominent local rancher and early settler in Fallbrook, purchased the hotel and renamed it the Ellis. The period of Ellis ownership was the hotel's heyday as it played host to county civic and business events and drew vacationers from across the nation and the world.

Hotel registers from the years 1911-1918 showed guests representing 24 states and the Territory of Hawaii, several Canadian provinces, and Japan. A joint meeting of northern San Diego County chambers of com-

An undated photo of the Ellis, a prominent Fallbrook landmark from 1889 to 1958
Fallbrook Historical Society

merce drew 500 attendees. Railroad and water authority officials were regular guests, along with traveling theater troops, salesmen, and vacationing dignitaries

Among those often staying at the hotel or just stopping by to spend some time on its veranda were so-called "remittance boys." As one former Fallbrook resident familiar with the situation described it, it was the custom of the English gentry "to give the eldest son property and the youngest a given income each year." Some young "remittance boys" migrated to Australia, Canada, or the United States. According to the *Fallbrook Enterprise,* some who were "ranching" in the Fallbrook area used to "ride into town on their horses" and sit on the front porch of the Ellis Hotel to "pass the time of day."

The remittance boys figured in a humorous anecdote involving the hotel in 1912 which was recalled years later in the local press. A Mr. Stintin, his wife and young son were driving from San Diego to Santa Monica. Encountering a heavy rainstorm which caused the fabric roof of their car to leak, they pulled into Fallbrook to ride out the storm.

The Stintins "were ushered into the bridal suite in the cupola" which was "grandly furnished with a fourposter bed featuring a down mattress, and on the highly polished floor was a white bear rug."

The Stintins "enjoyed the dining room, where everyone had their meals family style around a long table on the ground floor."

Their stay lasted two days. Cars were still rare enough that Stintin's Locomobile attracted a lot of attention. The newspaper reported that "the remittance-men and their friends relaxing on the veranda of the hotel all asked for rides and Stintin obliged."

On the day of his departure, Stinton was presented with "$12 in payment for the Locomobile rides." He must have appreciated the hospitality because Stinton ultimately moved to Fallbrook.

Hotel owner William Ellis died in 1923. His widow Adelle Ellis operated the hotel for two more years before selling it in 1925 to Joseph Smarr. Smarr and his wife ran the hotel until his death in 1929. Mrs. Smarr ran the hotel only three more years, closing it to visitors in 1932. She continued to live in six rooms of the hotel until 1957, but apparently never reopened it for guests.

In 1957 Mrs. Smarr moved to Needles to live with her daughter, and the now empty hotel quickly fell victim to vandalism. In November of that year, 35 young people converged on the abandoned building on a late-night "ghost-hunt" and were arrested by sheriff's deputies for disturbing the peace after complaints by neighbors. The incident spurred Mrs. Smarr to order the building torn down. Demolition began early in 1958.

An article in the January 2, 1958 *San Diego Evening Tribune* said "Most Fallbrook residents would like to see the place preserved, but the practical ones see no chance of it." Costs to restore the badly vandalized building were apparently too great.

Just a few years after the old hotel's demise, public interest in historic preservation began to grow across the country as new public laws and private organizations formed to preserve many old buildings. The Ellis may have had a chance for rebirth if it had survived just a few more years. Today it can be appreciated only through the archives of the Fallbrook Historical Society and through a detailed scale model on display there.

The telephone comes to town

On July 1, 1897, telephone service came to the city of Escondido. The Escondido telephone exchange was only the second in all of San Diego County at the time. Service had begun in the city of San Diego in 1881, according to an account in the *Times-Advocate* in 1962.

The article described San Diego County in those days as "sparsely developed with only a few small concentrated centers of population." Those population centers were "isolated, self-contained economic and social units with extensive undeveloped territory between them."

In Volume II of his book, *History of San Diego: 1542-1908,* historian William E. Smythe described the San Diego Telephone Company, which had introduced phone service in the 1880s, as "not incorporated, but...operated as a mutual affair, as the telephone business was thought to be in an experimental stage."

In 1890, the San Diego Telephone Company was succeeded by San Francisco-based Sunset Telephone and Telegraph which began efforts to connect San Diego with the rest of California. In June, 1897, the *San Diego Union* announced completion of the phone line as far as Escondido. A. H. Beach was the first local telephone agent, presiding over a small switchboard in a rented office on Grand Avenue near Lime Street (Broadway).

The Escondido telephone office in 1905, showing (left to right) Ed Hatch, Harry Smith, Clarence Anderson, Olga McCorkle, Pearl Trembly and a man identified only as Mr. Johnson.
Pioneer Room /Escondido Public Library

The 1899 phone directory, showing the Escondido listings, covered the entire Pacific Coast. It listed 18 telephones in the Escondido exchange, used by 17 customers. One customer, Dr. J.V. Larzalere, had separate phones for his office and residence. Most of the other subscribers were businesses, including the Escondido Hotel, druggist W. H. Baldridge, B.D. Churchill and Company's flour mill and Graham & Steiner's department store.

Local phone agents had to balance the tasks of staffing the switchboard, maintaining equipment and building a customer base for a business still in its infancy. A 1979 *San Diego Union* article noted that most of the early telephone agents "had a second income and ran the business out of their homes simply because they had no more than a handful of customers."

In 1900, the number of subscribers dropped to 10 when the manager, a man named Norton, was unable to fulfill his job due to illness. Then a new manager, Ed Hatch, took over. Hatch, then 48 years old, fit the jack-of-all-trades profile for phone managers of the time. The 1900 U. S. Census lists his occupation as painter. Other contemporary and historical accounts list him as running a bakery and the local Wells Fargo agency as well as the telephone office.

Within a year, Hatch increased the number of subscribers to 17 while running his office literally as a family business. A 1957 *Daily Times-Advocate* article stated Hatch "used his children, two sons and daughters, to operate the switchboard and help in running the business."

By 1905 the Sunset company had been acquired by Pacific Telephone and Telegraph. In Escondido the phone business had grown to the point where Hatch added the first non-family members to his payroll, lineman Clarence Anderson and operators Olga McCorkle and Pearl Trembly. They are shown in the accompanying photograph along with two lineman who worked out of the phone company's San Diego office. There were 23 telephones in the Escondido exchange.

The telephone business turned out to be a family affair for more people than just Ed Hatch. In 1955 the *Daily Times-Advocate* ran the 1905 staff picture and was contacted by then 75-year-old Olga McCorkle Kernick. The paper later reported that in addition to being a phone operator in Escondido from 1905 to 1908, she had married a fellow telephone company employee, Edward J. Kernick, a San Diego-based switchboard maintenance man whose voice she first heard "on a San Diego-Escondido long distance call."

The Old Richland School

Richland School, circa 1911. *San Marcos Historical Society*

The Old Richland School still stands on a wooded hill between Mission Road and state Route 78 in San Marcos. Located on what is now Woodland Parkway, it was erected as a one-room schoolhouse in 1889, built of redwood boards and square nails. A second classroom was added in 1890. One room housed grades one to four, the other five through eight.

The New England-style structure with its distinctive belfry was the first school in San Marcos to have a bell, according to Maryanne Cioe, librarian of the San Marcos Historical Society.

The school served the Richland area for nearly 70 years as the community grew and eventually became part of the city of San Marcos. Originally called the Richland School, it was renamed Old Richland School in 1962 after the construction of a new elementary school of the same name. Like many rural schools of its day, Old Richland also served as a community center and at times a church.

The school didn't have electricity or running water until the late 1930s.

Before then, kerosene lamps were used for evening events, and a windmill drew water from a nearby well.

The historical society archives contain reminiscences of former students who recalled the days of a small, tightly-knit rural community.

Louise Fulton Hard, a first-grader at the school in 1916-17, wrote about climbing the steep hill up to the schoolhouse with her classmates each morning, boys and girls going to their respective anterooms, and getting "a drink of water from the dipper in the water bucket." The tolling school bell meant "an hour to play before the bell rang again to call us in."

Old Richland's school bell figured prominently in a story related by former student Ida Lucas Dodge in a letter written in 1971, now in the possession of the historical society. She attended the school in 1914-15 along with her older sister Nellie Dodge.

Describing herself in the third grade as a "very shy" small-for-her-age loner, Dodge relates what happened one day when her teacher, Miss Fulton, asked her to ring the school bell signifying the end of recess: "I became so carried away by the fun of swinging up and down on the bell rope that when my sister came in to stop me, I had rung the bell twenty-four times!"Embarrassed "to the point of tears," little Ida went outside "to find everyone, even Miss Fulton, laughing hilariously!"

Al Wilson, who attended Old Richland School in the 1930s, later became an Escondido realtor. He spoke warmly of his years at the school to a *San Marcos Courier* reporter in the early 1960s. "The average kid didn't get lost in the shuffle" Wilson said. "A kid gets an identity in a small school."

In 1947 the old schoolhouse on the hill was closed after 58 continuous years of service. However, it was reopened in 1951 to house an overflow of second and third-graders from the Richmar Elementary School District.

The school was retired again in 1957. In 1966 the boarded-up building and eight surrounding acres were purchased by retirees John and Thelma Nichols, who remodeled the building as a home while preserving as much of the schoolhouse as possible. In 1984 Arie De Jong, a prominent local businessman, bought the property and continued to restore the schoolhouse structure and furnishings. In 1997 he opened the schoolhouse as a social hall for catered events.

Yet the building's metamorphosis was not finished. In 2002 it was leased by Delphi Academy, which converted it to a private school campus, offering kindergarten through third-grade classes. The old schoolhouse had come full-circle.

"A representative cowboy"

From the 1950s until his death in 1975, Valley Center was home to self-described "Representative Old Cowboy," Edgar "Ed" Wright, who had a ranch near Hillview Road in Valley Center.

On the occasion of his 83rd birthday in 1972, Wright gave an interview to The *Sentinel,* a local edition of a regional paper put out by *The Vista Press*. In that interview he talked of his life as a "representative cowboy," meaning an authentic working cowboy and later as a rodeo performer and circus clown.

Born in 1889 in Illinois, Wright grew up with horses, riding from his earliest days. Contracting tuberculosis as a child, he was sent to Wyoming for a cure. He recovered and was able to live out his dream of being a working cowboy on cattle ranches in Wyoming, South Dakota, Montana and Colorado in the first decades of the twentieth century.

"A representative cowboy," Wright told *The Sentinel* in 1972, "was one whom an owner of several thousand cattle could trust to literally represent him and his interest in taking care of his cattle."

Wright went on to describe the austere life of cowboys on the range who never had more than "a couple pair of Levis at one time" and slept on the ground using "their boots or sourdough coat for a pillow. The sourdough coat was a sheepskin-lined coat. The cook would wrap his sourdough in it so it'd raise; that's where it got its name."

At some point in his cowboy career Ed Wright began performing in rodeos and wild west shows. On permanent display in the Valley Center Museum is a saddle used by Wright "at every major rodeo, frontier show and fair for 20 years starting in 1915," according to a plaque put up by the museum.

Karen Spillman of the National Cowboy and Western Museum in Oklahoma City said Ed Wright was in the museum's computerized database as a "steer wrestler." The museum's photo collection lists shots of Wright participating in steer wrestling but also calf-roping and other events at rodeos in Dewey, Oklahoma, Pendleton, Oregon, and Sonora, Arizona between 1917 and 1932.

In her 1993 book, *Fearless Funnymen: The History of the Rodeo Clown,* rodeo historian Gail Hughbanks Woerner noted that as rodeos evolved from impromptu competitions among cowboys into professional events paying cash prizes and charging spectator fees, a support crew became essential to keep audiences entertained between acts. This support crew included the rodeo clown.

It wasn't unusual, Woerner wrote, for cowboys to become clowns or to double as clowns and to work not only rodeos and wild west shows but circuses as well. She briefly cites Wright as an "early competing cowboy" on the emerging rodeo circuit. Regarding his move into clowning, she quotes from a 1954 self-published biography, "The Representative Old Cowboy Ed Wright," keeping his colloquial way of writing: "They paid a good clown more money fer a show than a cowboy could make if he won, so I got me a jackass an' tried ta dress so I'd look like one myself. Well, it worked."

Woerner's book lists Wright as working as a rodeo clown during the years 1918-1925.

There is some limited documentation in the archives of the Valley Center Museum indicating that Wright worked in the 1920s as a clown with Ringling Brothers, Barnum and Bailey Circus.

Deborah Walk, Circus Archivist with the Ringling Museum in Sarasota, Florida, was not able to verify Wright's employment with the show, but added "that doesn't mean anything" because accurate employment records for the circus only date back to 1938 and circus programs in the 1920s didn't list clowns' names.

A cowboy's life was a wandering life and not always well documented. "You probably won't find much about him, but all the cowboys knew him," said Gail Lamb, former Valley Center Librarian and a pioneer researcher in local history who was also acquainted with Wright as a fellow-rancher in the late sixties and early seventies.

Ed Wright died in 1975 and is buried in Valley Center Cemetery. Inscribed on his tombstone is the same saying that used to hang on a sign at the entrance to Wright's ranch: "End of the Trail."

Harry Tassell: a do-er, not a talker

Tassel Road in Poway is named for Harry Tassell though the street name is missing the final "l." Tassell was a local rancher and school bus driver who was active in civic affairs. He played a role in Poway's transformation from an unincorporated, sparsely populated rural hamlet to the burgeoning city of today. Officials at the city of Poway couldn't explain why the street is spelled differently.

Tassell was born in Borden, Kent, England in 1885. He immigrated to the United States in 1907, sailing on the S.S. Caronia from Liverpool, arriving in New York on October 16 of that year. The passenger manifest for that voyage describes young Harry as 5 feet, 7 inches tall with fair hair and gray eyes. His ultimate destination was given as San Diego where he was joining an uncle living at 135 22nd Street.

Victoria and Harry Tassell, 1942
Poway Historical and Memorial Society

After arriving in San Diego, Harry met and married another English immigrant, Annie Mae Abbott. Between 1913 and 1924, they had four children: Alma, Irene, Gordon, and Mary Joyce.

Annie Mae Tassell died in 1927.

Harry Tassell worked as a carpenter while living in San Diego but had a strong desire to own land. He purchased ten acres in Poway and moved his family there in 1916. Tassell's ranch was in the Twin Peaks area, near Community Road and Norwalk Street, according to his daughter-in-law, Aileen Tassell, 80, of Escondido.

Mary Joyce Thomas, who is 81 and lives in San Leandro, recalls her father growing "grapes, oranges, persimmons, peaches and apricots," and owning "one riding horse, one plow horse, and a cow."

She has memories of Harry loading up a wagon with produce early in the morning to take over the Poway Grade to sell in San Diego. Asked if her father continued to practice carpentry in Poway, Mrs. Thomas could not recall him doing work for others but said he built the family's house and other buildings for the ranch.

In then-rural Poway, Mary Joyce and her siblings "roamed the countryside" on horseback. "I rode up to Twin Peaks and all over the valley."

A rough count of tracts from the 1930 United States Census for the southern part of Escondido Township, covering what is now the City of Poway, showed a population total of 367. Mary Joyce Thomas attended the three-room Pomerado School on Midland Road with grades one to three in one room, four to six in the second, and seven and eight in the third. Poway students had to go to Escondido for high school.

In 1932 Victoria Lott came to Poway from Arizona to take a teaching job. Two years later, she became Harry Tassell's second wife. In a 1974 interview published in the *Poway News-Chieftain*, she talked of Poway as "a close- knit community in those days. We planned community-wide Thanksgiving dinners and had a great time."

Harry and Victoria Tassell became active in Poway public life. Harry served on the school board and was the first Boy Scout leader in Poway. He was a founder of the Poway Chamber of Commerce and was chamber vice president at the time of his death.

Tassell was an original member of the Poway Municipal Water District board. The election for the board started the process that brought Colorado River Water to Poway in 1954. He was elected vice-president of the first board.

According to his daughter Mary Joyce, Harry Tassell "never talked much about what he did. He just did it." But she did remember him telling her, "We have to have water because Poway is going to become a suburb of San Diego."

When Tassell died in 1959, Poway wasn't yet incorporated, so he might not have foreseen that his community would become a thriving city in its own right. But his involvement with the water board helped make that outcome possible.

Harry's widow Victoria, who became Victoria Michels when she remarried in 1962, carved out her own place in Poway's history as well. On her retirement in 1971, she was the longest-serving teacher in the Poway school system. She was active in numerous community organizations including the Poway Historical and Memorial Society.

She died in 1996. Her name lives on in the Victoria Estates development, built by her second husband Al Michels near the site of the original Tassell homestead.

Pauma Valley

The tragedy of Rancho Pauma

In a 1987 *San Diego Union* article, Hugh Crumpler wrote, "The center of activity in Pauma Valley in 1846 was Rancho Pauma, owned by Jose Antonio Serrano."

The rancho was granted to Serrano in November 1844 by then-Alta California Governor Manuel Micheltorena, according to Robert Brackett's 1939 book, *History of San Diego County Ranchos.*

After California became part of the United States, "a claim was filed with the land commission November 1, 1852 and confirmed May 16, 1854," wrote Brackett. "It was patented August 29, 1871 to Jose Antonio Serrano, Blas Aguilar and Jose Antonio Aguilar."

Jose Antonio Serrano was the grandson of Francisco Serrano, who came to California with Junipero Serra in 1769. Blas Aguilar was Serrano's brother-in-law.

"This rancho lies on San Luis Rey River," wrote Benjamin Hayes in his diary in the early 1860s, "about 15 miles S.W. of Warner's rancho, 10 miles south of Temecula and 42 N.E. of the town of San Diego."

Hayes was a circuit-riding judge with social and political connections to many of the early California ranching families, including Serrano, so he knew Rancho Pauma well. "The river flows through it all the year and beyond as far as Pala," wrote Hayes, "and it has several fine creeks, with abundance of grass and choice oak and fine timber, in quantity three square leagues or 13, 317 acres. Its climate is pleasant the year round."

In his 1965 book, *Some Old Ranchos and Adobes,* Philip Rush described Jose Antonio Serrano as "a splendid horseman" who "took part in bull fights" and fought with the Californios at the Battle of San Pasqual in 1846.

Crumpler noted that the Pauma Indians "provided much of the labor needed to operate Pauma Rancho." He also noted that "relations between the Indians and the Californios had been strained from the time the Mexican government secularized the missions in 1834."

"Strained" may be putting it mildly. The Pauma, the original residents of the land, found themselves reduced to tenants, often treated worse than slaves by ranch owners and their overseers. Even decidedly Eurocentric historians of the last century like Rush couldn't totally avoid mentioning "the harsh treatment the Indians received from the settlers, ranch owners and padres."

That relationship between Rancho Pauma's owner and its indigenous residents was further complicated by the Mexican-American War as the United States entered the power struggle for control of the land. The war triggered the Pauma Massacre, the event most often associated with the rancho.

After the Battle of San Pasqual, Serrano had offered sanctuary on his ranch to 11 men and young boys who had fought with him in the battle. The group, including relatives and friends of Serrano, also brought their cattle, sheep and horses, hoping to avoid confiscation of the livestock by the American forces.

While Serrano and his family were at the Pala mission on business, a group of Pauma Indians gained access to the rancho adobe and seized the 11 men staying there. The captives were taken to the Warner Springs area. After some fruitless efforts at negotiation between Californio and Indian leaders, the captives were put to death.

In retaliation Californio leaders gathered a force which, joined by members of the Cahuilla Indians, took vengeance on the Pauma in what has come to be known as the Temecula Massacre. Some 100 Paumas were killed in that attack. Together, the events at Pauma and Temecula constitute two of the bloodiest massacres in California history.

Serrano and his family continued in possession of at least part of the rancho through 1871, as indicated by the 1871 patent. Over the next two decades parts of the ranch were sold off, with one-third of the acreage going to Judge Benjamin Hayes' son, J. Chauncey Hayes, and another third to Roman Catholic Bishop Amat.

In 1892 the ranch site was designated as part of the Pauma and Yuima Reservations.

Parts of Rancho Pauma, including the ruins of the Serrano adobe, are today included in a federally designated historic site, according to Juana Majel-Dixon of the Tribal Legislative Council of the Pauma Band of Mission Indians. Pondering a painful history with many lessons still to be learned, she said "This is the beginning of a long journey of discovery in America's history with the Pauma-Yuima Band."

Valley Center

General store and more

It was, in the words of one owner, the "social hub" of Valley Center. The building, which stood at the corner of Valley Center Road and Old Road, served the community for decades as a general store, post office, library, and finally as a liquor store. When the structure was destroyed by fire in 2002, it was the oldest continuously used commercial property in Valley Center. Remnants of the building live on today at the Valley Center History Museum.

Records in the archives of the Valley Center Historical Society trace the structure back to at least the early 1920s. It was then a simple one-story wooden structure. Prior to 1923 a general store and post office had been operated at Valley Center and Lilac Roads by Clara and George Shelby. Evidence in the museum archives indicates that the latter building, erected in the early 1900s, may have been moved to the corner of Valley Center Road and Old Road in the early 1920s, but the information is not conclusive.

When Clara Shelby died in 1923, her daughter Nell Chandler was appointed the new postmaster. *Once Upon A Time in Valley Center*, a booklet compiled in 1992 by the Valley Center Historical Society, includes part of a letter written by Nell Chandler stating that she and her husband Fred Chandler "moved to the new store and Post Office, which was on the corner of Valley Center Road and Old Road. Mr Chandler and I operated the business there for twenty years."

A 2001 *Union-Tribune* article noted that the general store "sold everything from food to clothes. The family also sold eggs, fruit and vegetables produced by local farmers."

In 1943, the building was acquired by Walter and Martha Pilz who had moved to Valley Center from northern California. Their son Hal Pilz was away in the service but returned after the war to help run the business.

Hal Pilz, 85, said his parents originally moved to Valley Center to retire,. However, when the store became available, his father, who had run retail businesses in Los Angeles and the San Francisco Bay area, saw development possibilities. Within a few years Walter Pilz had doubled the size of the store, adding another room, extending the original "false-

The Valley Center General Store,1930. *Valley Center Historical Society*

front" façade, and building an adobe ice house and garage.

The store dispensed gasoline from two pumps out front and "in the middle was an old glass pump that dispensed kerosene, because electricity was not a common thing," Hal Pilz told the *Union-Tribune* in 2001. "There were lots of places out there in Valley Center that were using kerosene lamps at night."

In a recent interview, Hal Pilz also noted that "there were only about four active telephones in Valley Center when I came back from the war." Valley Center's only public telephone was on the porch of the general store. Hal Pilz would often have to drive on unpaved roads to deliver phone messages. He utilized a mail route map hanging on the store's wall to find people's homes.

The end of World War II brought a wave of veterans who bought land in Valley Center while working in urban areas like Los Angeles. They would come on weekends to develop their local property, then head back to the city during the week.

"You wouldn't believe how many times I drove down to Western Metals in San Diego for barbed wire," said Pilz. Barbed wire and fence posts were in great demand, he said. So were war surplus army tents. The weekend residents bought them for storage of supplies during the week, according to Pilz.

Under the Pilz family the general store also resumed service as a branch of the county library. Under the Chandlers from 1923 to 1929 the store had housed one shelf of books, changed monthly by a county employee. Then the library was moved to a local restaurant until 1946, when it came back to the general store. The Pilz family maintained five shelves of books there.The store served the community as a branch library until 1961 when the county bookmobile began making regular visits to Valley Center.

In 1956 William McMann purchased the property, converting it into the Corral Liquor Store. It remained a local landmark until 2001. That year it was threatened with demolition due to the planned widening of Valley Center Road. Efforts by the McMann family and local historic preservationists to have it moved were ended by a fire in December 2002.

Remnants of the building have found a new life at the Valley Center History Museum. Wood salvaged from the burned building was used to construct a reproduction of a circa 1862 homesteader's cabin which is on permanent display at the museum.

When Rancho Bernardo was still a ranch

Rancho Bernardo today is a bustling community of homes and businesses with a population (as of 2006) of 45,000. But Donald Daley, Jr. can remember a different RB.

"You know the golf course and the inn?" Daley asked, referring to the signature resort and golf course that form the historic heart of the planned neighborhood. "When I was a kid it was an alfalfa field. We had 60 acres of alfalfa. It was gorgeous."

Donald Daley's family was the last of a line of working ranchers tracing back to Don Jose Snook who received the original Mexican land grant for Rancho San Bernardo in 1842 and built a large cattle and sheep-raising operation. Over the years successive owners including James Hill, Colonel Ed Fletcher and William Henshaw grew grain and raised livestock on the ranch.

The original rancho grant totaled 17,763 acres. Over the decades parts were subdivided or sold off. The 6,000 acres forming today's Rancho Bernardo were a working ranch until 1961. George Daley began working the property under a lease in the 1920s. He was a member of a pioneer ranching family which at that time owned properties in Escondido and Jamul.

George Daley bought the property outright in 1943. On his death in 1957, the ranch passed to his nephews, Donald and Lawrence Daley.

The ranch was bounded on the north by Lake Hodges, on the south by Rancho Peñasquitos, on the east by the Bernardo Winery, and on the west by 4S Ranch.

"As late as the 50s and early 60s it was pretty rugged country," recalled Lawrence Daley in a 1986 *San Diego Union* article, "with no roads except farm trails, and we had to use horses instead of cars most of the time."Lawrence Daley died in 2002.

That same 1986 article noted that the land now occupied by Bernardo Heights Country Club had been range land for cattle. Fields of barley covered what would become the site of the Bernardo Heights Community Center.

The original livestock kept by the Daleys consisted not of cows but horses and mules, according to Donald Daley, Sr. In a 2006 interview, Daley, who died in 2007, said his uncle George originally started leasing the property to raise horses and mules "for farming and construction. During World War I, a lot of work around San Diego was done with mules and horses," said Daley. "You raised oat hay which was good for horses and mules," he said. The cattle came "later on," he said.

Daley recalled a drive of horses and mules over the old Highway 395 bridge at Lake Hodges on the way to the family's Escondido ranch. He said there were also cattle drives along the then two-lane road, but they ceased after the 1930s. After that, according to Daley, livestock would be trucked rather than driven on the hoof for grazing at Escondido, Jamul, or on land in the Miramar area that his family leased for grazing.

While some articles in local papers over the years referred to both wheat and barley being grown on the ranch, Donald Daley, Sr. said that barley was grown, but not wheat.

"We raised oat hay on the red lands and barley on the adobe hills where you could thresh it," Daley said.

In 1952 Lawrence Daley built a new ranch house. That house still stands today, privately owned but no longer by the Daleys, almost totally surrounded by the Rancho Bernardo Golf Club.

It was in that house that the agreement was signed in 1961 between the Daley brothers, Harry Summers and W.R. Hawn which led to the development of Rancho Bernardo as a planned community While some cattle continued to graze in parts of Rancho Bernardo into the late 1960s, the land's future was in houses, condominiums, schools, shopping centers and office parks.

The Oden family: triumphs and tragedies

The life of George John Oden, a German immigrant who was an early settler in the Twin Oaks Valley, demonstrates the triumphs and tragedies of the immigrant experience.

Most of the details of his life come from *The Oden Family Biography,* an undated manuscript written by Gustav Dellmann, Oden's son-in-law. Dellmann died in 1967. His manuscript is in the archives of the San Marcos Historical Society.

George Oden was born in Prussia in 1848. He was a baker in the city of Essen when, in 1873, he married Elizabeth Anna Homer.

In 1882, the couple and their five children emigrated to the United States, settling in Chicago. Another child, Katherine, was born in 1884.

Oden soon joined a group of other German immigrants in purchasing land in California for the proposed Colony of Olivenhain. Promotional brochures promised the immigrants a rich, well-watered soil that was already yielding an abundance of olives.

Decades later, in a local newspaper article written on the occasion of her 87th birthday, Oden's widow told a reporter, "When we arrived April 19, 1885, we found only two olive trees and bare hills of sagebrush. We were victims of one of the early California land swindles."

Some families chose to remain in Olivenhain. The Odens chose to look elsewhere. They joined four other families living in an abandoned adobe barn four miles to the east from which the men fanned out over the county looking for work. Work was scarce. George Oden finally found work sixteen miles away on the farm of Gustave Merriam, who had been homesteading in the Twin Oaks Valley since 1875.

The Oden family on its Twin Oaks farm in the late 1880s.
San Marcos Historical Society

For a number of weeks Oden walked sixteen miles every Sunday to Twin Oaks, where he worked until the following Saturday evening when he would walk home to his family. Then Merriam offered him 160 acres just west of the Merriam farm. Oden took over the acreage and began the painstaking task of clearing the land for planting.

The family biography notes that most of Oden's acreage was covered with brush "which had to be cleared with a mattock, or grubbing hoe, before planting." Oden planted wheat, barley and oats along with some fruit trees and vegetables. He dug a well 30 feet deep.

The soil proved rich, yielding abundant crops. In 1887 George and Elizabeth welcomed another child, Charles, into the family.

The Oden farm had a stand of oaks covering about an acre. The six Oden children gave names to individual trees: the "nanny tree" where a milk goat had been tethered; the "lizard tree" because of the lizards crawling on it.

The oaks were the setting of many Sunday picnics which attracted other German immigrants from surrounding communities. The immigrants helped each other out: "Much of the labor requiring more than one man was done on a barter basis among the Germans in that area. A days work given was returned in kind."

Education was important to the family. *The Oden Family Biography* reports that they were influential in creating the first school district at Twin Oaks, of which George was one of the first trustees.

By 1892 Oden, then 44, was successful enough as a farmer to begin planning for a bigger house for his family. But his life was cut short in a tragic accident in March, 1893. A heavy rain loosened the soil around the rock perimeter of his well. When some of the rocks became loose Oden rigged a windless so he could be lowered into the well to repair the damage. Suddenly the entire mass of rock collapsed into the well, killing him. The family biography reported that "the entire countryside came to help," using lumber to shore up the well to recover the body.

Oden left behind a 39-year old widow and six children. Elizabeth Oden, with the help of her two oldest sons, George and Fred, built the new house her husband had planned and continued to run the family farm. In 1896 she married Alvin Frohberg. She lived until 1948. Friends held a dinner for her at San Marcos Recreation Center in 1941 on her 87th birthday, honoring her as one of the area's pioneers

"The best of my life"

When Henry T. Sandford died in 1937 at the age of 83, his obituary in the *San Diego Tribune* saluted him as a "pioneer resident and builder of San Diego." Sandford was, according to obituaries in both the *Tribune* and the *San Diego Union*, a city building inspector for a number of years before going into business as a building contractor credited with constructing more than 200 San Diego homes.

Not mentioned in either of those obituaries were the six years he spent as foreman of Rancho Los Peñasquitos, a period Sandford fondly recalled as one of the best times of his life.

The San Diego County Parks and Recreation Department, with the City of San Diego, runs the Rancho Peñasquitos Canyon Preserve. The department has documents and photographs of Sandford and his family in its archives. The materials include a short, handwritten account of his time on the ranch, written sometime in the 1920s.

"Henry T. Sandford was a versatile man typical of his era," said San Diego County Historian Lynne Christenson. At various points in his life Sandford worked as a farmer and rancher, merchant, newspaper worker, contractor and builder as well as a carpenter and a building inspector.

Born in Wisconsin in 1854, Henry Topping Sandford came to California with his parents in 1877, first settling in Healdsburg. There Henry met and married Belle Leonard. They had two children, Seth Charles and Alice Esther.

Sandford and his family came to San Diego County in 1888. The following year he was appointed superintendent at Rancho Los Peñasquitos by then-owner Colonel Jacob Shell Taylor. Taylor, a wealthy Texas and New Mexico cattleman and founder of Del Mar, acquired the 7,000-acre ranch from previous owner George Alonzo Johnson in the early 1880s, according to a brief history compiled by the county.

"During the land boom of the 1880s, Taylor settled into the ranch house and ran a direct phone line and stage between Peñasquitos and Del Mar," the history stated. With three business partners, he attempted to subdivide the ranch, "but the deal fell through in the crash of the late 1880s and Taylor sold his holdings in 1889 to early day land speculator Adolph Levi."

Henry Sandford moved into the ranch house to run the operation for its absentee owner. The house the Sandfords occupied had started out as a one-room adobe built in 1823 by Captain Francisco Maria Ruiz, first grantee of Rancho Santa Maria de los Peñasquitos. The modest house underwent a considerable expansion in the 1860s by then owner George Alonzo Johnson. A July 1892 article on the ranch in the *San Diego Sun* described the house as the Sandfords knew it: "It has fourteen rooms and surrounds three sides of a court around which run verandas."

The article said Sandford "understands his business thoroughly and expects to make the ranch profitable for its owners."

Henry's brief history of his time on the ranch, less than ten pages, was written on stationary bearing the letterhead "H. T. Sandford, Contractor and Builder." The letterhead also bears a blank line for the month and day and "192_" for the year.

His account provides some interesting details about ranch operations. "I think it was in 1893," he wrote, "the terrible dry year when cattle died on the hills of starvation, that we cared for 850 head of cattle and 300 head of horses and colts, and all came through finely."

His descriptions of citrus production on the ranch illustrated the ups and downs of the ranching business: "In the middle nineties the company put out 5,200 lemon trees in one grove but early frosts killed every tree." On the other hand, the ranch's five-acre orange grove "bore so well that I shipped three carloads of fruit at a time, three times in one season, realizing about $2,700 in returns."

According to Sandford the ranch was a prime destination for visitors, especially hunters. Some 1,000 acres of brush on and around Black Mountain in the ranch's northeastern corridor "constituted the finest quail hunting domain I ever heard of," wrote Sandford. "We entertained hunters of worldwide experience and many corroborated my judgement in this matter."

He described hosting "many globetrotters, magazine writers and people of wealth and prominence, and it made life worthwhile to be able to meet such delightful people as we often encountered there."

"Altogether it was a lovely house and I can never forget that I enjoyed several years of the best of my life there," Sandford concluded.

Homer Williams: He helped bring water to Poway

The area of Poway encompassing the subdivisions of Valle Verde, Green Valley and Silver Saddle was once all Valle Verde Ranch. Originally carved out of the Rancho San Bernardo grant, Rancho Valle Verde was a still-functioning but run-down ranch until the arrival of David Homer Williams in 1948. Williams gave the ranch new life. He also played a pivotal role in the transformation of Poway from an unincorporated rural area to a thriving city.

Williams—all his friends knew him as Homer—was born in 1909, one of eight children born to a Tennessee farming family, according to his son Bob. Bob Williams, a real estate consultant and still resides (as of 2008) in the last Poway house his parents lived in.

When Homer was nine his family moved to Oklahoma. "It was tough going" there for Homer's cotton-farming father, said Bob Williams.

Around 1925, at the age of 16, Homer and an older brother headed for California. There Homer started working on the Murphy Ranch in Whittier tending horses and mules. He worked there for 18 years, rising to general manager. While working there in 1933 he married Elizabeth Nichols. They raised two children, Robert, born in 1938, and Julianne, born in 1943.

From Murphy Ranch, Williams moved to La Habra where he became general manager of the Imperial Ranch. When he came to Poway to become general manager of Valle Verde in 1948, the 1,280-acre property was in a state of disrepair, Bob Williams said. The ranch's longtime owner, Dr. William Wickett, a physician and investor from Fullerton, had sold the ranch shortly after World War II. The buyer reneged on payments and neglected to work the land, leading Dr. Wickett to foreclose.

Within a year of Homer's arrival, Wickett was so impressed with the improvements that he offered his general manager a one-percent ownership share in the ranch for every year Homer remained on the job.

The two men developed a strong friendship, according to Bob

Members of the Poway Municipal Water District at a groundbreaking for an aqueduct, January 1954. Homer Williams is second from left in the front row.
Poway Historical and Memorial Society

Williams, so much so that Wickett "left almost all the decision-making with regards to the ranch up to my dad," he said.

Williams added grains to the ranch's existing citrus operation.

"Most of the citrus was on the hills," said Williams. Low-lying areas, which were too cold for citrus crops, were planted in barley and oats instead. The ranch sold a lot of oat hay to the Del Mar Racetrack.

"He was a good farmer," said Williams of his father. "He knew how to raise hay so that it was properly cured to insure its sweetness but still retain the grain, which is where the food is."

From 1949 until his death in 1994, Homer Williams recorded the monthly rainfall at the ranch in a little black book. His records were so meticulous that in the early 1960s, Williams remembered his father getting a phone call from the National Weather Service asking to make copies of the book. The service sent Homer Williams a new rain gauge as thanks.

The lack of a steady water supply became critical in the Poway Valley by the early 1950s. It was during this period that Homer Williams approached his friend Dave Shepardson, suggesting they go to the Metropolitan Water District of Southern California for help.

The district told Williams and Shepardson they couldn't deal with individuals, only organizations. Out of that meeting evolved the Water Committee of the Poway Chamber of Commerce. That committee in turn evolved into the Poway Municipal Water District which brought Colorado River water to Poway in 1954.

In a June 2006 interview, Don Short, who was the chief engineer on the 1954 project, said, "As a person who was there on the spot at the time, I have nothing but the greatest respect for those individuals who are truly responsible for bringing water to Poway and those individuals are Dave Shepardson, Homer Williams and Harry Frame."

Homer Williams served as secretary of the water district's board of directors from 1954 to 1958 and as president of the district from 1958 to 1960.

A steady water supply made Poway more desirable for residential development, and at Valle Verde as at other Poway ranches, farming began giving way to housing subdivisions. Homer Williams teamed with Wickett, Short and Shepardson to form the Valle Verde Ranch Company which developed the first phase of Valle Verde Estates in 1955.

Homer Williams was not through with farming, though. In the early 1970s, at the age of 62, he took up the offer of his friends, the Daley family, to clean up and manage 200 acres of avocados on the Daleys' Escondido ranch.

"He did that until the day he died," Bob Williams said.

The Vista Community Center was completed in 1941, built of adobe bricks, by volunteers.
Vista Historical Society

Vista

Built from the soil

Community members literally built it with their own hands. It was first known as the Vista Recreation Center, later as the Vista Community Center.

Vista was a growing agricultural community in 1939 when a Committee for the Recreation Center was established. "Townspeople were unanimous in expressing a need for a center, both for the kids and for many adult committees and groups," wrote Harrison and Ruth Doyle in their 1983 book, *A History of Vista.*

Earlier in the 1930s, community members had built a softball field with their own funds, volunteer labor and materials donated by local businesses. Volunteerism swung into action once again to build a recreation center on that same field at 160 Recreation Drive.

A committee was gathered consisting of Charles Mull, Sr., then manager of the Vista Irrigation District, School Superintendent Sherman Freeman, and housewife Grace Haymaker. Money for construction was raised "mostly from donations and benefits," according to *A History of Vista.*

The actual construction was done literally "from the soil," in the words of Luz Duran in a 2006 interview. Duran, who died in 2008, was one of the original community members who built the center out of adobe bricks, fashioned of mud mixed with straw right on the site. Luz Duran and his brother Tony, along with brothers J. G. and Dan Lara, were in charge of the construction site.

Luz Duran had come to Vista with his family as a 10-year-old in 1925. He started "helping carpenters as an apprentice. That's where I learned my trade." After World War II, he and his brother Tony started a construction company that would go on to build many of Vista's major buildings including the Elks Lodge and the Avo Theater.

About the recreation center, Duran recalls townspeople using their bare feet to stomp on the mud/straw mixture like Italian winemakers stomping grapes. He emphasized, as do the Doyles in *A History of Vista,* that the original construction was done primarily by members of Vista's Latino community.

The Doyles wrote that Vista School Superintendent Freeman "declared a one-day holiday of the schools and asked all male students to go to the Recreation Center with picks and shovels." Female students prepared food and beverages "and the boys put in the entire day" working at the site.

At one point a heavy rainstorm flooded much of the site, and some work had to be done over. But by 1941 community members had completed a rectangular adobe consisting of a large main meeting room, a kitchen and rest rooms. The main meeting room included a fireplace built with donated tile from Italy.

Duran, while pointing out the predominant role of Latinos in building the center, added that it was used by everyone in the community.

According to *A History of Vista,* "The Vista Community Association, during the two decades before Vista was incorporated in 1963, was the nearest thing here to local government—something concerned townspeople, being governed by the County Board of Supervisors 45 miles away, were feeling in need of."

Upon its completion, the center became a meeting place for many of Vista's early clubs and associations. Over the years, alterations were made, turning the rectangle into an "L," to meet the ever-growing community's demands.

Annemarie Cox, Program Coordinator for the San Diego Archaeological Center, is a 20-year Vista resident and was Director of the Vista Historical Society Museum from 1994 to 2002. She recalls the building as "a community center in the truest sense. It served the entire socioeconomic and cultural diversity of Vista." On any given night, Cox noted, the center might simultaneously host meetings of a bonsai class, a Korean martial arts group, and Alcoholics Anonymous. "At ten o'clock at night the place was still buzzing."

The building continued to be used as a community center until it was demolished in 2000 as part of a redevelopment project.

Home run king from Escondido

He was the home run king of baseball before Babe Ruth. He was also raised in Escondido and was the first San Diego county native to make it in big league baseball.

Clifford Carlton Cravath, better known as "Gavy" Cravath, rewrote the record books for power hitting as a right fielder for the Philadelphia Phillies from 1912 to 1920.

Gavy Cravath baseball card photo dated 1915
Pioneer Room/Escondido Public Library

Born in 1881, Cravath had roots in two of the county's earliest settler families. His father Augustus ranched in the Bernardo, Bear Valley and Poway areas before becoming Escondido's first mayor in 1888. His mother Kate was the daughter of Zenas and Eliza Sikes, pioneer settlers in what now forms the southern part of Escondido.

Cravath starred in both baseball and football at Escondido High School, graduating in 1899. He started playing baseball in 1902 with a San Diego team in the California League. A year later he was signed by the Los Angeles Angels of the fledgling Pacific Coast League. It was during this period that Cravath got his nickname, hitting a drive so hard in one game that it killed a sea gull in flight. The cries of "gaviota" (sea gull) by some Spanish-speaking fans were taken up as a chant by the rest of the crowd, and the young star came to be called "Gavy," (rhyming with "savvy"). Sportswriters wrote it with a double-v but Cravath himself is said to have preferred "Gavy."

In 1907 Cravath was voted the league's Most Valuable Player. The following year he was offered a major league contract by the Boston Red Sox. Two established stars, Tris Speaker and Harry Hooper, played in Boston's outfield, and Cravath got little playing time. Brief stints the next season with Chicago and Washington never really gave him a chance to prove himself.

In 1910 Cravath was back in the minor leagues with the Minneapolis Millers. The next season he led the American Association in batting with a .363 average, in doubles with 53, and in home runs with 29. His home run total was the most of any player in organized baseball at that time.

His outstanding year won Cravath another chance in the majors, as the Philadelphia Phillies acquired his contract for the 1912 season. He took advantage of the second chance. Over the next eight seasons, Cravath led or tied the National League in home runs six times. His total of 24 homers in 1915 was the highest ever for a major-league season up to that time. Cravath also led the league in runs batted in twice, with 128 in 1913 and 115 in 1915.

Bill Swank, a baseball historian from San Diego who has studied Cravath's career, wrote that "his home run and RBI percentages were the highest of the dead ball era." The "dead-ball" era was the pre-1920 period when opposing pitchers could legally doctor baseballs.

Gavy Cravath challenged the conventional wisdom on hitting, which emphasized hitting the ball on the ground to advance runners. He once told a reporter, "Short singles are like left-hand jabs in the boxing ring. A home run is a knockout punch. There is nothing that will take the backbone out of a pitcher like a home run."

His style may have led the way for Babe Ruth, who hit 29 home runs in 1919, surpassing Cravath's single-season major-league record. Cravath's career home run total of 119, once considered "unbeatable," was passed by Ruth in 1921.

Cravath's hustling action on the basepaths also contributed to rule changes. During one game, caught in a rundown between second and third with the infielders lobbing the ball back and forth, Cravath grabbed the ball in mid-lob, threw it into the stands, and raced home. A subsequent rules change made this action illegal.

Gavy Cravath's major league career was relatively short since he was 31 when he caught on with the Phillies. During his last two years with the team he was a player-manager. After two more years of managing and scouting in the minors, Cravath retired from baseball. He moved to Orange County, where he sold real estate and served as a justice of the peace for 36 years. He died in 1963.

In 1985 Gavy Cravath was inducted into the Breitbard Hall of Fame in the San Diego Hall of Champions Sports Museum. Baseball historian Bill Swank and Norm Syler, former executive director of the Escondido Historical Society, have led a campaign, so far unsuccessful, to get Cravath into the Major League Baseball Hall of Fame at Cooperstown, New York.

North County Historical Societies, Museums and Libraries

These facilities are all open to the public, but hours vary and are subject to change. It's advisable to call ahead.

Escondido History Center
321 N. Broadway
Escondido CA 92025
760-742-8207/www.escondidohistoricalsociety.org

Escondido Public Library, Pioneer Room
247 South Kalmia Street
Escondido, CA 92025
760-839-4315/www.ci.escondido.ca.us/library/pioneer

Fallbrook Historical Society
260 Rocky Crest Road
Fallbrook, CA 92028
760-723-4125/www.fallbrookhistoricalsociety.com

Cupa Cultural Center
35008 Pala Temecula Road
Pala, CA 92059
760-742-1590

Poway Historical and Memorial Society
14114 Midland Road
Poway, CA 92074-0019
858-679-8587/www.powayhistoricalsociety.org

Guy B. Woodward Museum
645 Main Street
Ramona, CA 92065
760-789-7644/www.woodwardmuseum.org/

Rancho Bernardo Historical Society Museum
Bernardo Winery
13330 Paseo Del Verano Norte
San Diego, CA 92128
858-487-1866/www.rbhistoricalsociety.org/

Rancho de los Peñasquitos
12020 Black Mountain Road
San Diego, CA 92129
858-484-7504
San Diego County
Department of Parks and Recreation
Website: www.sdparks.org

San Diego Historical Society
Museum of San Diego History
Casa de Balboa Bldg., Balboa Park
1649 El Prado, Suite # 3
San Diego, CA 92101
619-232-6203
www.sandieghistory.org/museum_of_san_diego_history.html

San Marcos Historical Society
270 W. San Marcos Blvd.
San Marcos, CA 92069
760-744-9025

Valley Center History Museum
29200 Cole Grade Road
Valley Center, CA 92082
760-749-2993/www.valleycenterhistory.org/

Vista Historical Museum
1315 Hot Springs Way, Suite 110
Vista, CA 92084-1032
760-630-0444
www.geocities.com/vistahistoricalmuseum/vista/home.htm
(As of this writing, the museum was planning a move to a new location, but the phone number and email address will remain the same. Be sure to contact them before visiting.)

Further resources

Lime Street School

Ryan, Frances B., "Early day grammar schools," *The News-Reporter,* February 12,1987.

"District history," from website of Escondido Union School District, www.eusd4kids.or/history.htm .

Ryan, Frances Beven, *Early Days in Escondido,* Escondido, Frances and Lewis Ryan, 1970, p. 71.

Daley, Howard, portion of manuscript in Pioneer Room, Escondido Public Library.

"Escondido celebrates," *Escondido Times,* September 15, 1905.

"Escondido schools," *Escondido Times,* September 13, 1907.

"Danger warning given by teachers," *Escondido Advocate,* May 7, 1909.

Ball, Neil, "Escondido fair, harvest ball set," *San Diego Union,* October 5, 1991.

Telles, Paul, "Escondido centennial," *San Diego Tribune,* September 29, 1988.

LaFee, Scott, "Progress menaces old bandstand," *San Diego Tribune,* April 26, 1988.

Obituary of Bryant Howard Daley, *Times-Advocate,* December 13, 1962.

Hawk, Steve, "The family that owned the land that turned to gold," Times-Advocate, January 15, 1984.

The McFeron story

"B.G. McFeron, Jr., scion of Poway pioneers," *San Diego Union-Tribune,* June 24, 1993.

Walker, Julie, "Poway's pioneers remember 'Jimmy' McFeron," *Poway News-Chieftain,* September 28, 1978.

Van Dam, Mary, *As I Remember Poway,* Poway, Poway Historical and Memorial Society, 1985, p. 115.

"Gus McFeron, Poway rancher, dies at age 85." Copy from archives of Poway Historical and Memorial Society.

Dining, dancing and fishing at Lake Hodges

Dare, Martino, "3 Lake Hodges bridges have spanned the decades," *Bernardo News,* October 18, 1990.

"Big change at Lake Hodges," *Daily Times-Advocate,* May 20, 1924.

"Catfish and bass planted," *Daily Times-Advocate,* June 7, 1924.

"Grand opening of Lake Hodges Pavilion," ad, *Daily Times-Advocate,* June 7, 1924.

"Was night of many dances," *Daily Timse-Advocate,* June 9, 1924.

Perkins, Eloise, "Old Hodges bridge," *Times-Advocate,* January 25, 1968, clipping from Pioneer Room.

Obituary for John E. Daley, *Daily Times-Advocate,* October 9, 1943.

Buskirk, Nick and Shirley, *Escondido: Then and Now,* Escondido, Heritage Publishing, 1993, p. 51.

McGrew, Alan B., *Hidden Valley Heritage: Escondido's First 100 Years,* Escondido, Blue-Ribbon Centennial History Committee, 1988.

The stars of Valley Center

Davidson, Helene, "Valley Center Celebrities," manuscript submitted in 2004 to archives of Valley Center History Museum.

The oldest Protestant church in Escondido

Berk, Lucy, "Donated land for churches drew settlers to Escondido," *San Diego Union-Tribune,* July 18, 2004.

Celebrating Our Centennial: 1886-1986, booklet produced by First United Methodist Church.

110th Anniversary: 1996, booklet produced by First United Methodist Church.

The little old schoolhouse

Seff, Marsha Kay, "Bonsall: Pastoral and Upscale," *San Diego Union-Tribune,* March 6, 1994.

Fleming, Lorell, "Bonsall district leaders seek community's help to move old schoolhouse," *North County Times,* June 2, 2007.

Funk, Virginia, and other members of the Landmarks and History Section, Bonsall Woman's Club, *The Little Old Bonsall Schoolhouse,* published 1984.

Camp Vista

"Roosevelt's Tree Army: A Brief History of the Civilian Conservation Corps," from website of National Association of CCC Alumni, www.ccc-alumni.org/history1.html .

Farina, John, "Monument dedicated to conservation corps," *San Diego Tribune,* October 22, 1984.

"Work begins on 15 CCC buildings," *Vista Press,* July 18, 1935.

"Conservation plans ready to function," *Vista Press,* November 28, 1935.

"New assignments at CCC Camp change officer personnel," *Vista Press*, February 13, 1936.

"Improving CCC camp educational facilities," *Vista Press*, February 20, 1936.

"Benefits offered to young men by CCC" and "Broad plan adopted for recreational activities at CCC," *Vista Press*, March 19, 1936.

"Soil conservation camp doing good work here," *Vista Press*, March 26, 1936.

"CCC aviation class graduates," *Vista Press*, January 4, 1940.

Escondido Hotel: A luxury destination

Ryan, Frances Beven, *Early Days in Escondido*, Escondido, Frances and Lewis Ryan, 1970, pp. 47-66.

Perkins, Eloise, "Hotel was center of early Escondido social life," *Escondido Daily Times-Advocate*, July 9, 1972.

Perkins, Eloise, "Escondido Hotel," *Escondido Daily Times-Advocate*, June 15, 1966.

Escondido Land & Town Co., "Escondido! The new colony of San Diego County, (full-page ad), *Escondido Times*, January 20, 1887.

Author unknown, "The new bus for the Escondido Hotel arrived on Friday last...(part of general news column), *Escondido Times*, March 29, 1888.

Author unknown, "The hotel addition is nearly finished..." (part of general news column), *Escondido News*, 5/3/1888, p. 1.

Author unknown, "Hotel arrivals," *Escondido News*, May 3, 1888.

Fox, Robin, "The Escondido Hotel," *Heritage Walk Quarterly*, published by the Escondido Historical Society, Spring 2004.

Olive days

Rivers, Don, "The Olive Industry of Fallbrook," essay originally published in the *Fallbrook Village News* October 1, 1998, copy in archives of Fallbrook Historical Society.

"Olive industry rapidly grows," *Fallbrook Enterprise*, March 24, 1911.

"Red Mountain Ranch," *Fallbrook Enterprise*, March 24, 1911.

"Scale pest discussed by citrus grower," *Fallbrook Enterprise*, May 6, 1911.

"The olive scores again this year..."*Fallbrook Enterprise*, January 31, 1913.

"Dr. Charles Pratt, founder of local fruit industry, passes," *Fallbrook Enterprise*, March 6, 1931.

"Shipment of first car of olives from new factory," *Fallbrook Enterprise*, March 9, 1917, transcript from archives at Fallbrook Historical Society.

Halloran, Art, "Old Cannery: A patriotic effort fades from memory," *Fallbrook Enterprise*, August 3, 1978, transcript in archives of Fallbrook Historical Society.

"Historical timeline for Fallbrook, CA," from Fallbrook Historical Society website, http://home.znet.com/schester/fallbrook/history/timeline.html.

An immigrant's dream

Enges-Maas, Mary, "Prohoroffs gone, but not forgotten," *San Marcos Courier*, October 17,1988.

Ma, Ken, "Higher learning hatched from two million chickens," *North County Times*, September 19, 2004

Snider, Julie, "Death of a chicken farm," *Times-Advocate*, September 29, 1985

Patriarch of Palomar Mountain ranchers

Beckler, Marion, *Palomar Mountain: Past and Present*, Palm Desert, Desert Magazine Press, 1958, pp. 10-15, 24, 27.

Wood, Catherine M., *Palomar: From Tepee to Telescope*, San Diego, Frye & Smith, 1937, pp. 39-42.

Lepper, Ruth, "Life at the lake is a job for Henshaw concession owners," *San Diego Union-Tribune*, September 24, 2003.

Strege, Dave, "Plenty of country in this club," *Orange County Register*, September 5, 2006.

"Colfax Founders Day, September 29, 2007," Palomar Mountain News website, www.mypalomarmountain.com/mendenhallbergman/page 3.html.

Silk and sunshine

Patterson, Ray, "City's silk-producing past left legacy," *San Diego Union-Tribune*, October 29, 2000.

Cordry, George, "Silk mill plays prominent role in San Marcos history," *San Marcos Reporter*, August 15, 1984, clipping from archives of San Marcos Historical Society.

Haskins, Roy, "Silk mill weaves through SM history," *North County Times*, November 22, 2000, clipping from archives of San Marcos Historical Society.

Gray, Donly, "Fate blocked San Marcos as silk center," *Escondido Times-Advocate*, 5-part series, May 22-May26, 1966, clippings from archives of San Marcos Historical Society.

"Silk culture," *Daily San Diegan*, October 13, 1891, clipping from archives of San Marcos Historical Society.

"The silk industry," *San Diego Union*, January 1, 1894, clipping from archives of San Marcos Historical Society.

Karp, David, "The fruit of broken dreams," Los Angeles Times, January 19, 2000, clipping from archives of San Marcos Historical Society.

"The San Marcos Silk Mill," manuscript written in 1992 by former mill worker Henry Frank Kehn, from archives of San Marcos Historical Society.

"The secret of sericulture," from Silkroad Foundation website, www.silkroad.com/artl/silkhistory.html .

"History of sericulture," website of *Cultural Entomology Digest*, www.insects.org/ced1/seric.html .

Melancton Barnett: business man and civic leader

1898 letter of Evelyn Wile to Melancton Barnett, from "Schools" folder of Barnett file, Guy B. Woodward Museum archives.

1912 textbook receipt, from "Schools" folder of Barnett file, Guy B. Woodward Museum archives.

1916 state hunting license for Melancton Barnett, from "general" folder of Barnett file, Guy B. Woodward Museum archives.

1910 certificate of membership for Melancton Barnett on San Diego County Fair Commission, from "general" folder of Barnett file, Guy B. Woodward Museum archives.

Letter of Ed Fletcher to Melancton Barnett, January 4, 1917, from "Correspondence" folder of Barnett file, Guy B. Woodward Museum archives.

Letter of Fletcher to Barnett, August 27, 1916, from "Correspondence" folder of Barnett file, Guy B. Woodward Museum archives.

Letter of Fletcher to Barnett, November 8, 1917, from "Correspondence" folder of Barnett file, Guy B. Woodward Museum archives.

Lepper, Ruth, "Historic Ramona Town Hall Remains Closed," www.ramonajournal.com, June 13, 2005.

"Lake Hodges Dam History," www.hodgee.com .

Wickham, Gertrude Van Rensselaer, *The Pioneer Families of Cleveland: 1796-1840*, Cleveland, Evangelical Publishing House, 1914, pp. 299-300.

A lot of history in a little church

Lepper, Ruth, "Old redwood church sanctuary still in use," *San Diego Union-Tribune*, March 31, 2002.

Van Dam, Mary, *As I Remember Poway*, Poway, Poway Historical and Memorial Society, 1985.

Notes on church history from Mrs. Forest Paulson, congregation member, in October 1963, Archives of the Poway Museum.

Kordela, Donna, "Community is proud of historic church," *Sentinal/Poway*, August 13, 1977, Archives of the Poway Museum.

Russell, Kathlyn, "Old house of worship to 'retire,'" *San Diego Union* April 11, 1987, Archives of the Poway Museum.

You knew you were home when you saw the tepee

"The tepee: a lost landmark," Robin Fox, *Heritage Walk Quarterly*, Volume 27, No. 2, Summer 2000.

"Toppled tepee has sweet history," Dan Bennett, *North County Times*, July 10, 1996.

"Local landmark simply whimsical," Kathryn Bold, *Escondido Times-Advocate*, October 4, 1987.

"End of an era: the tepee is gone," editorial, *Escondido Times-Advocate*, December 22, 1977.

"Time takes its toll of a hilltop tepee," Dave Ballard, *San Diego Union*, November 10, 1977.

"Time squelches tepee plans," Eloise Perkins, *Escondido Times-Advocate*, May 23, 1977.

"Teepee on hill landmark but also vandals' target," *San Diego Union*, February 20, 1966.

"Conversion of teepee to memorial still under study of CC,", *Escondido Times-Advocate*, March 14, 1957.

"Wigwam of whim: the unique Escondido landmark," Ted Krec, *Westways*, March, 1957.

"Massive tepee still an enigma," Alfred Jacoby, *San Diego Union*, October 28, 1956.

"Builder of teepee dies in Idaho," *Escondido Times-Advocate*, October 20, 1956.

"'Tepee is interesting Escondido Landmark; was planned as home," *Escondido Times-Advocate*, January 9, 1942.

Castle in the canyon

Entry on Isaac Frazee on AskART, online database on American artists. www.askart.com .

Alexander, Brian, "Scottish-style castle reigns over Valley Center ranch," *San Diego Tribune*, September 19, 1991.

Author not given, "Peace blessings form theme of pageant," *San Diego Union*, August 22, 1915, page obscured. Copy of clipping from files of Valley

Center History Museum.

Author not given, "Lark Ellen sings at Indian pageant," *San Diego Union,* August 23, 1915.

"Spotlight," *San Diego Union-Tribune,* July 23, 2005.

Factsheet, "Historic Home: 29360 Pamoosa Lane, Valley Center." Valley Center Historical Society.

The town of Barham

Author unknown, "Old Markets," manuscript from archives of San Marcos Historical Society.

Carroll, William, "San Marcos: A Brief History," San Marcos, Coda Publications, 1975, pp. 9-11, 13-15, 23, 26-27, 45-46.

Manuscript, "Information on James Barham and John H. Barham from *San Diego Union,* 1882-1885, compiled by Roy Haskins for the San Marcos Historical Society.

Excerpt from interview of Thomas Barham, son of John H. Barham, given in 1980 to Ruth Lindenmeyer of San Marcos Historical Society.

Obituary of John Henry Barham, 5/23/1930, newspaper name not shown, copy of clipping from archives of San Marcos Historical Society.

The Cupeño Expulsion

Introduction to the Cupeño People, pamphlet published by the Cupa Cultural Center.

Hill, Jane H and Nolasquez, Rosinda, *Mulu'wetam: The First People,* Banning, California, Malki Museum Press, 1973, pp. 43-51, 180-182.

Donaldson, Milford Wayne, on behalf of E Clampus Vitus, *Cupeños Trail of Tears,* pamphlet prepared to accompany dedication of commemorative plaque at Warner Springs Ranch.

"The Expulsion," history section of Pala Band website, www.palatribe.com.

Brett, Brigid, "North County's Trail of Tears," *North County Times,* December 15, 2004.

Lepper, Ruth, "Pala tribe working to preserve its tradition," *San Diego Union-Tribune,* May 26, 2002.

Barfield, Chet, "Heartfelt homecoming:Tribe visits village its ancestors were forced to leave," *San Diego Union-Tribune,* May 2, 2003.

Elmer Field: a skilled mechanic

Binder on Elmer Field, including family materials donated to the Escondido Historical Society and transcripts of oral histories gathered by the society, located in Pioneer Room of the Escondido Public Library.

Obituary of Elmer Field, *Times Advocate*, November 7, 1995.

Obituary of Anne Fjeld, *Times Advocate*, January 3, 1979.

Obituary of Martin Fjeld, *Times Advocate*, January 20, 1965.

Gustafson, Greg, "Tower has new home at Escondido park," *San Diego Union-Tribune*, May 6, 2005.

Griffin, Vern, "Park signals a new commitment," *San Diego Tribune*, March 1, 1990.

Griffin, Vern, "Pastoral park to be apple of Escondido's eye," *San Diego Tribune*, June 24, 1988.

Sickler Brothers Mill

Christenson, Lynne Newell, Ph.D., with Ellen Sweet, "Sickler Brothers Pala Mill in Wilderness Gardens Open Space Preserve: County Historic Landmark Nomination," report published August 3, 2005 by County of San Diego, Department of Parks and Recreation.

Jones, J. Harry, "History beckons from obscure park," *San Diego Union-Tribune*, April 20, 2006.

Naiman, Joe, "Sickler Brothers Mill designated as county historic site," *Fallbrook/Bonsall Village News*, 6/15/2006, p. A13.

Water made the difference

Doyle, Harrison and Ruth, *A History of Vista*, Vista, 1983 Hillside Press

"Population doubles," *Vista Press*, February 17, 1928.

Website, Vista Irrigation District,
http://www.vid-h2o.org/aboutus/ourhistory.asp.

"History of the Vista Irrigation District," manuscript provided by VID.

Fallbrook's lost landmark

Fallbrook Historical Society, "Early Hotel," *Fallbrook In Review*, Volume 2, Summer 2000 Edition, pp. 1-9. Quarterly journal of Fallbrook Historical Society.

Ellis, Maie, *Pictorial History of Fallbrook 1880-1920*, self-published 1978, pp. 146-154.

Factsheet on hotel from archives of Fallbrook Historical Society, undated.

Transcriptions of Ellis Hotel registers, 1911-1918, in archives of Fallbrook Historical Society.

Stone, Joe, "Ancient hostelry doomed by owner," *San Diego Evening Tribune*, January 2, 1958.

The telephone comes to town

C.R. (Chuck) Love, "Escondido telephone exchange was second in county," *Times-Advocate*, August 23, 1962.

Smythe, William E., *History of San Diego: 1542-1908*, Volume II, San Diego, The History Company, 1908, pp. 436-437.

San Diego Union, December 24, 1890, item in "Local Intelligence" column.

San Diego Union, 3/15/1897, item in "Local Intelligence" column.

San Diego Union, June 21, 1897, item in "Local Intelligence" column.

"Telephone company has interesting history in Escondido during 60 years,"*Daily Times-Advocate*, July 15, 1957.

"Phone operator of 1905 recalls early day here," *Daily Times Advocate*, October 28, 1955.

Twelfth Census of the United States (1900), Enumeration District 177, pp. 9-10, household of Edward Hatch and p. 12, household of William McCorkle.

The Old Richland School

"Old Richland School," factsheet compiled by San Marcos Historical Society, August 26, 2003, in San Marcos Historical Society archives.

"Old Richland School," Historic Resources Inventory, San Marcos Historical Society, November 5, 1979, copy in San Marcos Historical Society archives.

Hard, Louise Fulton, "Lunch with the blue-eyed boy," *San Marcos Star*, October 2, 1980, copy in San Marcos Historical Society archives.

Oral history interview with Louise Fulton Hard, September 17, 1978, from San Marcos Historical Society archives.

Letter of Ida Lucas Dodge to John and Thelma Nichols, September 6, 1971, now in possession of San Marcos Historical Society.

"Former student recalls '3R' days at old Richland," *San Marcos Courier*, March 1963, clipping copy from San Marcos Historical Society archives.

"Teacher, husband restore schoolhouse into a home," *San Diego Union*, November 27, 1982. Copy in San Marcos Historical Society archives.

Duckett, Robert, "Dairyman keeps the past alive by rebuilding a school," *Escondido Times-Advocate*, April 13, 1990. From San Marcos Historical Society archives..

"The Old Richland Schoolhouse," brochure for social hall, circa 1997, from San Marcos Historical Society archives.

"New private school opens in San Marcos," *The Paper*, May 16, 2002, San Marcos Historical Society archives.

Griffin, Vern, "Old schoolhouse a lesson in history," *San Diego Tribune*, April 16, 1987.

Ball, Neil, "Schoolhouse is a lesson in history," *San Diego Union-Tribune*, January 17, 1993.

Walker, Cheryl, "Ding Dong Bell: one-room school house rings in special occasions," *San Diego Union-Tribune*, April 2, 1998.

"A representative cowboy"

Wennerberg, Herb, "'Old Cowboy Ed' still punching the trail," The Sentinel, March 2, 1972, clipping from archives of Valley Center History Museum.

Woerner, Gail Hughbanks, *Fearless Funnymen: The History of the Rodeo Clown*, Austin, Eakin Press, 1993, pp. 1-65, 205.

Wright, Edgar, *The Representative Old Cowboy Ed Wright*, self-published, 1954, from bibliography of Woerner book.

Website of National Cowboy and Western Museum, Oklahoma City, OK, www.nationalcowboymuseum.org.

Website of Cheyenne Frontier Days Old West Museum, Cheyenne, Wyoming, www.oldwestmuseum.org.

Harry Tassell: a do-er, not a talker

Transcript of interview August 26, 2005 by Cecilia Burr of Poway Historical and Memorial Society with Aileen and Cynthia Tassell, daughter-in-law and granddaughter of Harry Tassell, from archives of Poway Museum.

Transcript of phone interview by Cecilia Burr of Poway Historical and Memorial Society with Mary Joyce Thomas, daughter of Harry Tassell, August 9, 2005, from archives of Poway Museum.

Ship manifest for voyage of SS Caronia from Liverpool to New York, October 1907 from Ellis Island website, www.ellisisland.org .

Birth information on Harry Tassell from birth, marriage and death indexes for England and Wales, obtained from Ancestry.com website (www.ancestry.com).

Birth and death records for Alma, Irene and Gordon Tassell obtained from Social Security birth and death records on Ancestry.com website (www.ancestry.com).

Excerpt from Fifteenth Census of the United States: 1930, for Enumeration District 37-15, (southern Escondido Township, which is today

Poway), obtained from Ancestry.com website (www.ancestry.com).

Information on coming of Colorado River water to Poway obtained from historical sketch on City of Poway website, (www.ci.poway.ca.us/history.html).

Obituary for Harry Tassell, clipping with newpaper name and date cut off from archives of Poway Museum. Death date independently established as April 15, 1959.

Whalen, Judy, "Memories of early Poway related," *Poway News-Chieftain*, September 26, 1974, clipping from archives of Poway Museum.

The tragedy of Rancho Pauma

Rush, Philip S., *Some Old Ranches and Adobes*, San Diego, Neyenesch Printers, 1965, pp. 68-72.

Brackett, Robert W., *History of San Diego County Ranchos*, San Diego, Union Title Insurance and Trust (reprint of book originally printed in 1939).

Hayes, Benjamin, "Pioneer Notes from the Diaries of Judge Benjamin Hayes, 1849-1875," pp. 286-288, from Library of Congress website, www.memory.loc.gov.

"What was the Pauma Massacre?", SD Chicano History, website www.-rohan.sdsu.edu/dept/mas/chicanohistory/chapter04/c04s07.html.

Crumpler, Hugh, "Pauma Valley's peacefulness belies its bloody past," *San Diego Union*, October 10, 1987.

Crumpler, Hugh, "Will the captives die?" *San Diego Union*, October 15, 1987.

General store and more

Patterson, Ray, "Historic store faces wrecking ball," *San Diego Union-Tribune*, April 29, 2001.

Repard, Pauline, "Two-alarm fire destroys landmark in Valley Center," *San Diego Union-Tribune*, December 5, 2002.

Walker, Cheryl, "Phone display shows how community kept in touch," *San Diego Union-Tribune*, July 31, 2004.

Berk, Lucy, "New branch latest chapter in Valley Center's library history," *San Diego Union-Tribune*, December 22, 2002.

Valley Center History Museum & Historical Society in partnership with the Friends of the Valley Center Library, *Once Upon A Time in Valley Center*, 1992, pp. 10-12.

Urrea, Yvette, "Building lost in fire was a VC landmark," *North County Times*, December 6, 2002, clipping from archives of Valley Center History Museum.

When Rancho Bernardo was still a ranch

"Rancho Bernardo: Community Overview,"website of San Diego North Chamber of Commerce, http://www.sdncc.com/communities/RanchoBernardo .

Patterson, Ray, "Home on the rancho," *San Diego Union-Tribune,* February 18, 2001. Clipping from archives of Rancho Bernardo Museum.

Daniels, Dwight, obituary for Lawrence Daley, *San Diego Union-Tribune,* November 5, 2002.

Scott-Blair, Michael, "Rancho Bernardo: not just retirees and red-tiled roofs," *San Diego Union,* August 1, 1991.

Raffer, Sharon, "The house that Daley built called RB's first hacienda," *Bernardo News,* May 27, 1993. Clipping from archives of Rancho Bernardo Historical Society Museum.

"Roundup day traditions fading fast with spread of civilization in Bernardo," *Daily Times-Advocate,* April 27, 1969. Clipping from archives of Rancho Bernardo Historical Society Museum.

The Oden Family: triumphs and tragedies

Manuscript, *The Oden Family Biography,* by G.H.P. Dellmann, undated, in Oden Family file at San Marcos Historical Society.

Author unknown, "Friends honor pioneer woman," September 29, 1941. Clipping in Oden family file at San Marcos Historical Society.

"Mrs. Frohberg rites tomorrow," January 14, 1948. Newspaper name not shown; clipping in Oden family file at San Marcos Historical Society.

Perkins, Eloise, "Olivenhain founded on false hopes," *Times-Advocate,* February 6, 1977. Clipping from Pioneer Room, Escondido Public Library.

Carroll, William, *San Marcos: A Brief History,* San Marcos, Coda Publications, 1975.

"The best of my life"

"Rites are set for pioneer builder," *Evening Tribune,* September 16,1937.

"H. T. Sandford, 83, dies; formerly employee of city," *San Diego Union,* September 16, 1937.

Sandford, H. T., "Los Peñasquitos Rancho," archives of San Diego County Department of Parks and Recreation.

San Diego County Department of Parks and Recreation, "Rancho Peñasquitos: A Brief History," factsheet.

Porterfield, W. H., "The back country: improvements at Las Peñasquitas (sic) Ranch," *San Diego Sun,* July 16, 1892, page number obscured, copied from archives of San Diego County Department of Parks and Recreation.

Homer Williams: He helped bring water to Poway

Rossi, Vincent Nicholas, "Water was key to Poway's growth," *San Diego Union-Tribune*, July 9, 2006.

Obituary for David Homer Williams, *Poway News Chieftain*, October 6, 1994.

Built from the soil

Doyle, Harrison and Ruth, *A History of Vista*, Vista, Hillside Press, 1983, pp. 46-48, 63-66.

Home run king from Escondido

Magee, Jerry, "Cravath had clout in the deadball era," *San Diego Union-Tribune*, December 21,1999.

Jenkins, Logan, "Local home-run king faces last crack at Cooperstown," *San Diego Union-Tribune*, September 16, 1998.

Savage, Jeff, "Gavvy Cravath, oldtime homer king, will be honored," *San Diego Union-Tribune*, January 14, 1985, C-6.

Clippings file, Pioneer Room, Escondido Public Library.

Escondido Historical Society Collection, Pioneer Room, Escondido Public Library.

Frances Beven Ryan Collection, Pioneer Room, Escondido Public Library.

McGrew, Alan B., *Hidden Valley Heritage: Escondido's First 100 Years*, Blue-Ribbon Centennial History Committee, Escondido, 1988.

Brochure, "The Sikes Adobe Farmstead," published by San Dieguito River Park, San Diego, CA.

"Gavy Cravath," plaque displayed in Breitbard Hall of Fame, San Diego Hall of Champions Sports Museum. Text provided by Steve Sloan, Curator.

Swank, Bill, "Before the Babe," *The Baseball Research Journal*, No. 29, 2000, p. 51.

Letter to Baseball Hall of Fame Veterans Committee from the Gavy Cravath Hall of Fame Nomination Committee, November 18, 1998.

James, Bill, *The Bill James Historical Baseball Abstract*, Villard Books, New York, 1988, pp. 88, 106-107.

Index

A

Abbot, Annie Mae, 60
Abernathy, Henry C., 34
Aguilar, Blas, 62
Aguilar, Jose Antonio, 62
Allyson, June, 10
American Silk Factors, 29, 30
Anderson, Clarence, 54, 55
Astaire, Fred, 10
Averill, Elise, 16
Avo Theater, 77
Avocado Capital of the World, 50

B

Balboa Park, 21
Baldridge, W. H., 55
Barham, 40, 41
  James, 40
  John, 41
  John H., 40
  Olley, 40
  Thomas, 40, 41
Barnett, Augustus, 31
Barnett, Melancton, 31, 32
Bartlett, Francis W. and Mary, 51
Battle of San Pasqual, 62, 63
Beach, A. H., 54
Bear Valley, 78
Beckler, Marion, 27
Ben Hur, 10
Benny, Jack, 11
Bergman, Arlie, 27, 28
Bernardo, 78
Bernardo Heights Community Center, 67
Bernardo Heights Country Club, 67
Bernardo Winery, 9, 67
Black Mountain, 72
Blunt, Donald, 9
Blunt, Herbert, 9
Bonsall, 15, 16
Bonsall Schoolhouse, 15
Borden, William Webster, 40, 41
Boston Red Sox, 78
Bower, W.M., 39
Bowron, Samuel, 34
Brackett, Robert, 62
Breitbard Hall of Fame, 79
Buena Vista Creek, 49
Buskirk, 7
Bussey, Norma Field, 45

C

Cahuilla Indians, 63
California Associated Olive Growers, 22
California State University San Marcos, 26
Carmody, M. J., 18
Carrol, William, 40
Cassou, James, 4
Chandler, Fred, 64
Chandler, Nell, 64
Christenson, Lynne, 71
Christenson, Lynne Newell, 47
Christian Endeavor, 34
Church, Harriett, 13
Churchill and Cassou, 45
Churchill, B.D., 55
Cioe, Maryanne, 56
Citizens Commercial Bank, 22
Civilian Conservation Corps, 17
Cole Grade, 10
Colfax, 27
Community Church of Poway, 33, 34
Congregational Church, 34
Conklin, Faith, 12
Consolidated Aircraft, 19
Cook, J. M., 22
Cook, Jean, 5, 6
Cooper, Gary, 10
Corral Liquor Store, 66
Cox, Annemarie, 77
Cravath
  Augustus, 78
  Clifford Carlton, 78

Gavy, 78, 79
Kate, 78
Crestview Manor, 6
Crumpler, Hugh, 62
Cupeño Cultural Center, 42
Cupeños, 42, 43

D
Daley, 75
Donald, 67, 68
George, 4, 67, 68
Howard, 3, 4
John, 8, 9
Lawrence, 67, 68
Daley Ranch, 3
Davidson, Helene, 11
Davis, Bette, 11
Del Mar, 32, 71, 74
Dellmann, Gustav, 69
Delphi Academy, 57
Delpy, Jules, 49
Dodge, Ida Lucas, 57
Dodge, Nellie, 57
Downey, John G., 43
Doyle, Harrison and Ruth, 76
Dunnotar Castle, 38
Duran, Luz, 76, 77
Duran, Tony, 76, 77
Dusing, Nettie, 16

E
Ecke, Paul, 25
Ehmke, Murray, 36
Ellis, Adelle, 53
Ellis, the, 51
Ellis, William, 51, 53
Escondido, 3, 4, 5, 6, 7, 8, 12, 13, 20, 21, 36, 37, 38, 44, 45, 46, 50, 54, 55, 57, 60, 61, 67, 68, 75, 78, 79
Escondido Land and Town Company, 20

F
Fallbrook, 22, 23, 51, 52, 53
Field
Dora, 44, 45
Elmer, 45, 46
Irma Ann, 45
Martha, 46
Norma Adele, 45
First United Methodist Church, 12, 14
Fjeld, Annie, 44, 46
Fjeld, Martin, 46
Fjeld, Martin and Annie, 44
Fletcher, Ed, 31, 32, 67
Frame, Harry, 75
Francis E. Willard Hotel, 51
Frazee, Isaac, 38, 39
Frazee, Isaac Jenkinson, 38
Frohberg, Alvin, 70

G
Gailey, Glenn, 30
Gang, Martin, 11
Garra Uprising, 42
Garra, Antonio, 43
Good, Bob, 34, 35
Graham & Steiner's, 55
Grant, Kirby, 10
Grape Day Park, 3, 4
Grass Valley, 27
Gray, Donly, 29, 30
Green Oak Ranch, 17
Griffin, Dr. John, 42
Guinn, J. M., 21
Gunn, Chester D., 49
Guy B. Woodward Museum, 31, 32

H
Haley, Jack, 10
Hard, Louise Fulton, 57
Harry Owens and His Royal Hawaiians, 9
Hatch, Ed, 54, 55
Hawn, W.R., 68
Hayes, Benjamin, 62
Hayes, J. Chauncey, 63
Hayes, Judge Benjamin, 43
Haymaker, Grace, 76
Henry, George S., 49
Henshaw, William, 67
Henshaw, William G., 31
Hercules, 10
Hill, James, 67

Hill, Jane, 42
Hilleary, Dr. Lewis, 33
Hinrichs, Suzanne, 37
Hinshaw, L. A., 8
Homer, Elizabeth Anna, 69
Hooper, Harry, 78
Horton, Alonzo, 27
Hotel Charlotta, 21
Houghtelin, A. L., 36
Houghtelin, Clair, 36, 37
Hurst, Glenn, 29

I
Imperial Ranch, 73
International Order of Good Templars Hall, 33

J
Jamul, 68
Jenkins, James, 43
Johnson, Connie, 36
Johnson, George Alonzo, 71, 72
Johnson, Mr., 54
Johnston, Captain A. R., 42
Jong, Arie De, 57
Jordan's Harmony Boys, 8

K
Kearney, General, 42
Kernick, Edward J., 55
Kernick, Olga McCorkle, 55
Knight, F.J., 49

L
Lake Henshaw, 49, 50
Lake Hodges, 7, 8, 9, 31, 32, 67, 68
Lamb, Gail, 59
Lara, Dan, 76
Lara, J. G., 76
Larzalere, Dr. J.V., 55
Leonard, Belle, 71
Lerner, Bob, 10, 11
Levi, Adolph, 71
Lewis, T. D., 33
Lime Street School, 3, 4, 83
Live Oak Canyon, 22
Loma Ranch, 22
Loring and Company, 31
Los Angeles Angels, 78
Lott, Victoria, 61

M
Majel-Dixon, Juana, 63
Marshall, William, 43
McCorkle, Olga, 54, 55
McFeron
  Budwin, 5, 6
  Daisy Arlene, 6
  Gershom, 5, 6
  Gus, 5, 63
  James, 6
  Nancy, 6
  Pauline, 6, 93
McFeron Rest Home, 6
McGilvriap, Donald, 39
McGrew, Alan, 8
McMann, William, 65
Mendenhall, Enos, 27, 28
Mendenhall, Sylvester Jacob, 28
Merriam, Gustave, 69
Merriam, H.S., 49
Methodist Episcopal Church, 12, 14, 33
Methodist Episcopal Seminary, 4
Mexican-American War, 63
Meyer, Martha, 45
Michels, Al, 61
Michels, Victoria, 61
Micheltorena, Governor Manuel, 62
Mills, Rachel Emily, 27
Minneapolis Millers, 79
Miramar, 68
Mission San Luis Rey, 42
Moosa Canyon, 38
Mount Fairview School, 15
Mount Palomar, 18
mulberry trees, 29, 30
Mull, Charles, 76
Murphy Ranch, 73

N
Naples Hotel, 51

National Association of CCC Alumni, 19
National Cowboy and Western Museum, 58
Native Daughters of the Golden West, 33
Nichols, Elizabeth, 73
Nolasquez, Rosinda, 42, 43
Norton, 55
Novarro, Ramon, 10

O

Oberon, Merle, 10
Oceanside Congregational Church 1, 33
Oden
  Elizabeth, 70
  Fred, 70
  George, 70
  George John, 69
  Katherine, 69
Ogburn, Amos Martin, 13
Old Richland School, 56
olive industry., 22
Olivenhain, 69

P

Pacific Coast League, 78
Pala, 43, 47, 62, 63
Pala Band of Mission Indians, 43
Pala Reservation, 43
Palomar Hospital, 20
Palomar Mountain, 27, 28
Panama-Pacific Exposition, 21
Paulson, Mrs. Forest, 35
Pauma Massacre, 63, 93
Pauma Valley, 10, 62
Pauma-Yuima Band, 63
Peace Pipe Pageant, 39
Philadelphia Phillies, 78, 79
Pico, Jose Antonio, 42
Pilz, Hal, 64, 65
Pilz, Walter and Martha, 64
Poway, 5, 6, 33, 34, 60, 61, 73, 74, 75, 78
Poway Chamber of Commerce, 61
Poway Municipal Water District, 61
Powell, Dick, 10
Pratt, Dr. Charles, 22
Prohoroff
  John, 24, 26
  Mary, 24
  Terenty, 24, 25, 26
Prohoroff Poultry Farm, 24, 25
Pryor, William, 21

R

Rainey building, 14
Ramona, 5, 31, 32
Rancho Bernardo, 7, 67, 68, 73
Rancho Los Peñasquitos, 71
Rancho Pauma, viii, 62, 63
Rancho Peñasquitos, 71
Rancho Rincon del Diablo, 20
Rancho San Bernardo, 32, 67
Rancho Santa Maria de los Peñasquitos, 72
Rancho Valle Verde, 73
Red Mountain Ranch, 22, 23
Reeves, Steve, 10
Richland school, 56, 57
Richmar Elementary School District, 57
Ringling Brothers, Barnum and Bailey Circus, 59
Rivers, Don, 22, 23
Rizzo, Ross, 9
Rock Springs School, 3
Rogers, Will, 10
Rubalcalva, John, 19
Ruiz, Captain Francisco Maria, 72
Rush, Philip, 62, 63
Ruth, Babe, 78, 79
Ryan Aeronautical, 19
Ryan, Frances Beven, 3, 21, 95

S

Sacramento, 27
Sample, Ed, 50
San Diego County Fair Association, 31
San Diego Telephone Company, 54

San Dieguito School District, 31
San Luis Rey River, 15, 42, 47, 62
San Marcos, 24, 25, 26, 29, 30, 40, 41, 56, 57, 69, 70
Sandford
  Alice Esther, 71
  Henry T., 71
  Henry Topping, 71
  Seth Charles, 71
Santa Fe depot, 20
Scott, Randolph, 10, 11
Serra, Junipero, 62
Serrano, Francisco, 62
Serrano, Jose Antonio, 62
Shelby, Clara and George, 64
Shepardson, Dave, 75
Short, Don, 75
Shubin, Jacob, 25
Shubin, Kathy, 25, 26
Sickler Brothers Mill, vii, 47, 48
Sickler, William A. and Marion M., 47
Sikes, Zenas and Eliza, 78
silk industry, 29
silk worms, 30
Sky King, 10
Smarr, Joseph, 53
Smarr, Mrs., 53
Smith, Harry, 54
Smythe, William E., 54
Snook, Don Jose, 67
Speaker, Tris, 78
Spillman, Karen, 58
Stintin, Mr., 52
Stone, Joseph and Amanda, 33
Stratton, W. A., 16
Striplin, Sam, 27
Summers, Harry, 68
Sunset Telephone and Telegraph, 54
Swank, Bill, 80
Sweet Leilani, 9
Sweet, Ellen, 47
Syler, Norm, 80

T

Tanner, 11
Tassel Road, 60
Tassell
  Aileen, 60
  Alma, 60
  Annie Mae, 60
  Gordon, 60
  Harry, 61
  Irene, 60
  Mary Joyce, 61
  Victoria, 58, 59
Taylor, Colonel Jacob Shell, 71
Temecula Massacre, 63
tepee, 28, 36, 37
The Wizard of Oz, 10
Thomas, Mary Joyce, 60, 61
Thomas, Virginia, 37
Trembly, Pearl, 54, 55
Turrentine, John Neil, 13
Twin Oaks Valley, 69
Twin Peaks Retirement Home, 6

U

United Church of Christ, 33, 35
University of Southern California, 12

V

Valle Verde Estates, 75
Valle Verde Ranch, 73, 75
Valle Vista Convalescent Hospital, 6
Valley Center, 10, 11, 38, 58, 59, 64, 65, 66
Valley Center General Store, 65
van Dam, Mary, 33
Vega, Lauro, 18
Vista, 6, 17, 18, 19, 49, 50, 58, 76, 77
Vista Community Center, 76
Vista Flume, 50
Vista Irrigation District, 50, 76
Vista Recreation Center, 76
Vista Soil Conservation Association, 18

W

Walk, Deborah, 59
Walker, Craig, 38
Warland, castle, 39
Warner Springs, 42, 43, 63

Warner, Juan Jose, 42
Wayne, John, 10, 11
Western Metals, 65
Westfall, George and Laura, 51
Westfall, Victor, 51
Wheeler, Nathan M., 13
Wickett, Dr. William, 73
Wilderness Gardens Open Space Preserve, 47
Wilderness Gardens Preserve, 48
Wile, Evelyn, 31
Williams
  Bob, 73, 74, 75
  David Homer, 73
  Guinn T. "Big Boy", 10
  Homer, 73, 74, 75
  Julianne, 73
  Robert, 73
Wilson, Al, 57
Wilson, W.H., 45
Woerner, Gail Hughbanks, 58
Wohlford, Alvin, 21
Women's Christian Temperance Union, 51
Wood, Catherine, 28
Woodward, Ken, 31, 32
Woreland Castle, 38, 39
Wright, Ed, 59
Wright, Edgar "Ed", 58

Y

Yaw, Ellen Beach, 39
Young, Loretta, 10